GW01287714

Moment of Truth

Redefining the CEO's Brand Management Agenda

Andreas Bauer
Björn Bloching
Kai Howaldt
Alan Mitchell

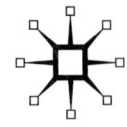
First published 2006 by
PALGRAVE MACMILLAN
Houndmills, Basingstoke, Hampshire RG21 6XS and
175 Fifth Avenue, New York, N.Y. 10010
Companies and representatives throughout the world

PALGRAVE MACMILLAN is the global academic imprint of the Palgrave Macmillan division of St. Martin's Press, LLC and of Palgrave Macmillan Ltd. Macmillan® is a registered trademark in the United States, United Kingdom and other countries. Palgrave is a registered trademark in the European Union and other countries.

ISBN–13: 978–1–4039–9896–5
ISBN–10: 1–4039–9896–5

This book is printed on paper suitable for recycling and made from fully managed and sustained forest sources.

A catalogue record for this book is available from the British Library.

A catalog record for this book is available from the Library of Congress.

10   9   8   7   6   5   4   3   2
15   14   13   12   11   10   09   08   07   06

Printed and bound in Great Britain by Cromwell Press

Contents

Figures

Tables

Acknowledgments

This book stands on the shoulders of two individuals who, while working for Roland Berger Strategy Consultants, first developed the methodologies and philosophy we outline: Tom Ramoser and Gerhard Hausruckinger. We thank them for their insight and expertise. Without them this book would have been impossible.

We would also like to thank the numerous clients who through a wide range of consulting contracts helped us test, develop, and extend the thinking, tools, and methodologies we describe. We would especially like to thank those clients who have been willing to share their learnings with a broader public through this book.

The book also benefited immensely from the input of a broader writing team, including, in alphabetical order, Rainer Balensiefer, Felix Dannegger, Adele Huber, Frederik Pohl, and Birgit Sponheuer, plus the research, organizational, administrative, and design support of Torsten Oltmans, Leonardo Leite, Doris Edenhofer, Anne Martin, Silke Peters, and Alexandra Woitakiewicz.

Thanks too to Stephen Rutt of Palgrave and Susan Curran of Curran Publishing Services for their editorial advice and support.

Any errors or oversights are, of course, our own.

Andreas Bauer
Björn Bloching
Kai Howaldt
Alan Mitchell

BOOK OVERVIEW

This book makes the case for a paradigm shift in brand management.

Brand management as practiced today is flawed. It starts at the wrong place: with the product rather than the customer. And it is hampered from start to finish by a series of endemic disconnects: between strategy and implementation, between different specialisms and departments, and between different 'styles' such as creative versus data-driven. The end result is ineffective strategy and inefficient implementation.

Organizations today need a new integrated, strategic approach to managing brands.

This integrated, strategic approach is by definition a cross-functional, organization-wide activity. It is the responsibility of the CEO, not the marketing director or brand manager.

THE MOMENT OF TRUTH

We need a new philosophy of branding.

Strong, differentiated brands cannot be built on the basis of product or service features or attributes alone. Every outstanding brand rests its foundations on a moment of truth when a customer recognizes that the brand has understood and addressed his or her values.

Brands are defined by the values of the people who buy them. These values determine both the functional benefits customers seek from products and services and the emotional attributes and associations they look for in brands.

It is not possible to build a strong brand without first connecting with the customer's values.

Values-based brand management starts by identifying and understanding different customers' values. It turns this under-

Introduction

Redefining the CEO's brand management agenda

THE CEO'S MOMENT OF TRUTH

Values-based brand management is a strategic exercise that influences the direction of the organization as a whole. It is inherently cross-functional in nature, involving operations, R&D, human resources, finance, as well as marketing. In short, it requires CEOs to embrace brand management as a cross-functional strategic process, and to organize and structure their companies accordingly.

---

standing into a common language – a unifying thread – which informs every aspect and detail of the brand building process from insight generation to strategy formulation to detailed implementation and execution.

Values-based brand management applies as much to B2B markets and brands as to consumer markets.

Because it is based on robust data, every step of the process is quantifiable and measurable. And it can be deployed to address all the major challenges of brand management, including positioning brands, reviewing brand portfolios and architectures, developing global brand platforms, identifying opportunities for innovation, fine-tuning the marketing mix, choosing between alternative creative communication executions, and tracking performance.

It can also be used to win internal staff understanding and engagement, to assess agencies' work, and to build business and brand alliances.

1 Setting the scene

Profitable top-line growth. Sometimes other priorities intervene. Sometimes cost cutting, restructuring, and retrenchment have to take center stage. Sometimes mergers, acquisitions, or divestments are top priority. But no CEO's thoughts ever stray too far from this *sine qua non* of business success. Ultimately attention always has to return to fundamentals: is the business making what customers want? Is it doing so profitably? How can it improve this performance?

In the end, that's what everyone in the business – shareholders, managers, employees, and suppliers – worries about.

Pursuing profitable top-line growth isn't a simple matter, however. It depends on a lot of things: operational and supply chain excellence, innovation, leadership, strategy, technology, and so on. One of these essential ingredients is branding.

The potential benefits of a strong brand – a clear, distinctive, and powerful reputation in the marketplace – have now been demonstrated, not just in traditional branding heartlands such as packaged goods, but in retailing, financial services, telecommunications companies, and many business-to-business (B2B) markets.

Strong brands help companies improve market share and margin, thereby generating the scale and cash flows that are the very essence of profitable top-line growth. By building trust they reduce risk and provide earnings stability and security. When and if a problem emerges, stakeholders are more willing to give a trusted brand the benefit of the doubt. Strong brands also open doors, making it easier to influence decision makers among potential business partners, in government, or the media. They provide a platform and create a focus for innovation and improvement. They help to clarify corporate priorities and behaviors. They act as recruiting sergeants for the best and brightest employees, motivating and informing their best efforts.

Considering these benefits as a whole, few businesses can afford to neglect the art and science of brand building – a fact that investors now understand very well. The stock market value of outstanding brand-building companies is accounted for primarily by the value of intangible assets such as their brands, not by tangibles such as property, plant, and machinery.

BRAND MISMANAGEMENT

But brand management has a problem. Many problems, in fact.

It's no longer enough simply to do the mechanics of 'branding' – to provide a catchy brand name, attractive and eye-catching product and packaging design, to 'own' a special color and associated imagery, carefully crafted advertising, and so on – because brands are becoming the new commodity. Nowadays, no self-respecting product or service can come to market without these basic mechanics of branding. Doing these things nowadays doesn't create anything special. People just expect it. It's standard practice which rarely differentiates the product or service in question. Indeed in today's mature and over-crowded markets most consumers are 'branded out': overloaded with brand messages, choice, and complexity. So by themselves, the day-to-day mechanics of branding rarely drive sales growth or deliver superior margins. To the contrary, increasingly the day-to-day mechanics are just a necessary cost of doing business.

At the same time, the bar for successful brand building is rising, with soaring stakeholder expectations. Consumers nowadays expect companies to demonstrate impeccable corporate social responsibility and ethical standards. Shareholders seek evidence that marketing expenditure does actually deliver worthwhile returns. Employees want to work for a company whose brands they believe in and that earns their friends' and families' respect. So on two counts – increased competitive pressure and rising expectations – CEOs need to improve the way their companies manage brands.

At the same time, competitive pressures are forever intensifying. It's very hard to make it to the top of the brand pecking order. It's even harder to stay there, as Interbrand's assessments of the value of the top global brands over the past five years demonstrates. Only two of

Table 1.1 Nowadays even maintaining a brand's value is a struggle

Changes in value of top brands 2000–05

Brand	Value ($ billion)		% change
	2005	2000	2000–05
Coca-Cola	67.5	72.5	−6.9
Microsoft	59.9	70.2	−14.7
IBM	53.3	53.2	0.2
GE	47.0	38.1	23.0
Intel	35.6	39.1	−9.0
Nokia	26.5	38.5	−31.4
Disney	26.4	33.6	−21.4
McDonald's	26.0	27.9	−6.8
Toyota	24.8	18.8	31.9
Marlboro	21.2	22.1	−4.0

Source: Interbrand.

the top ten have actually managed to increase their brand value faster than inflation.

In part, the data in Table 1.1 reflects the general business challenge faced by brands today. Changing markets, consumer expectations, and competitor activities mean yesterday's success formula won't necessarily come up trumps tomorrow. But they also reflect a deeper malaise. In too many companies today the underlying brand management process is broken: a frighteningly inefficient, even ramshackle mess. 'Brand management' is part of the problem, not part of the solution.

Table 1.2 sums up the 'dirty dozen' common problems that dog would-be brand managers today.

A disconnect between strategy and tactics

Many organizations display major disconnects between their overall business strategy and their brand and marketing strategies. Often marketing strategies and programs are driven more by short-term

Table 1.2 Brand management's 'dirty dozen'

1 Disconnect between strategy and tactics. Marketing just a 'bolt on.'

2 Erratic processes. Lack of consistency over time, across marketing mix.

3 Limited insight. Poor understanding of customer needs limits marketing potential.

4 Lack of analytical rigor. 'Gut feel' and lack of hard data lead to poor decisions.

5 Data incompatibility. Data sets that fail to 'speak' to each other; no 'big picture.'

6 No common language. Specialized departments (accounting, marketing) do not trust or understand each other.

7 Bureaucracy. Keeping to the rules more important than delivering results.

8 'Silo-itis.' The left hand does not know what the right hand is doing.

9 Brand narcissism. Meeting brand targets overshadows customer needs.

10 Confusing brand architecture. Lack of logic/coherence confuses customers.

11 Poor innovation. Too many line extensions, avoidance of risk.

12 Fence sitting. Risk-averse managers build 'blands' rather than brands.

tactical considerations than any long-term strategic plan, and the insights generated by marketers have no influence on what the rest of the company does: marketing is there simply to advertise and promote the stuff it has made. This happens when the brand is not really anchored in the organization and brand management is not seen as part of its core strategy; when the marketing department is separated organizationally and mentally from the rest of the company.

Erratic processes

Even in companies that have a clear strategy in place implementation may lack consistency across the entire marketing mix over time. Most brands need consistency to build momentum. But common syndromes such as 'new marketing director, new agency, new creative strategy' continually confuse customers, killing consistency and destroying momentum. Successful brand management depends on sustained, disciplined processes, which too many companies' marketing departments lack.

Limited customer insight

Outstanding brands are built on a foundation of deep insight into what drives and motivates different customer groupings. Today, however, too much market research is misconceived or misfocused, concentrating on relative trivialities, being driven more by internal politics than a genuine attempt to understand customers, or hampered in its design. The insights that are generated can't be translated into ongoing marketing programs that work well over time, across the entire marketing mix, from beginning to end.

Lack of analytical rigor

Many brand strategies are developed on the basis of marketers' 'gut feeling.' Many brand strategies – and especially advertising campaigns – are based on intuition and 'creativity,' with little hard data to inform or justify them. This makes it hard to quantify benefits and choose between alternative courses of action. Along the way, it undermines other departments' confidence in marketers and marketing. The end result is poor returns.

Data incompatibility

The other side of 'gut feeling' is too much 'information,' in the form of vast quantities of less-than-useful and often incommensurate data. Most companies invest vast sums in research, investigating a wide variety of consumer behaviors: consumption patterns, shopping behaviors, lifestyle, media consumption, attitudes, and so on. But because each research project is undertaken in isolation without a common data framework, marketers have no way to 'join up the dots,' to connect trends across markets, customer segments, territories, or categories. They are trying to complete a complex jigsaw puzzle without knowing what the final picture should look like, or even whether they have all the pieces. As a result practical, implementable brand programs with genuine strategic potential remain few and far between.

No common language

Different departments, such as operations, finance, and marketing, speak different languages, use different measures, and do not trust or understand each other. Priorities are determined more by internal power games than by consumer needs.

Bureaucracy

Many companies try to do 'marketing by numbers,' following a rule book that was written for previous times or other places. Budgets are based on historic criteria (such as what the budget was last year), and personnel promotions are linked to budget ('the bigger the budget, the more important the brand, the more important the person'). As a result organizations' marketing plans and processes become more inward looking rather than outward looking: the needs of the marketplace and opportunities for growth take second place. This is particularly dangerous when market conditions are changing rapidly, as with today's media and distribution channels.

Silo-itis

Often, there are deep disconnects within the organization between different silos delivering different elements of the brand promise. The advertising doesn't fit the promotion (in terms of message and/or execution). Customer service staff are not trained or empowered to treat customers the way the brand promises. Customers have different experiences with individual distribution channels, which fail to communicate with one another. As a result, brand consistency disappears to be replaced by customer confusion and disappointment.

Brand narcissism

The company 'falls in love' with its brand, not for the value it can generate for the company's customers, but for the business benefits it hopes it can generate for the company. The more the company focuses on achieving the potential business benefits of its brand plans, the less it focuses on customer needs and priorities. For example, many marketers spend more time and effort watching, and responding to, the competition than understanding customers. In companies with multiple-brand portfolios, brand managers often spend as much time and energy fighting each other for a share of the budget and management attention as they do identifying and meeting customer needs. A genuine customer focus could throw up huge potential for budget and initiative synergies.

Confusing brand architectures

Many companies allow their brand portfolios to grow like Topsy. Different brands end up competing with each other for the same customer segment or developing overlapping offerings, thereby confusing customers. This is a particular problem in companies that have grown rapidly by acquisition.

Poor innovation

Many companies are too slow, bureaucratic, and timid in their approach to innovation. While they are very good at 'refreshing' and tweaking existing brands, they are not good at delivering real innovations – the innovations that the market wants and that companies need in order to grow. Also, old product and brand deletion processes are rarely as rigorous as new product and brand introduction processes. As a result, brand portfolios become complex and confusing (see *confusing brand architectures*).

Fence sitting

Many companies say they want to build strong brands but actually they want to build 'blands': they want everyone to love them and buy them. By trying to appeal to everyone they end up appealing to nobody in particular. It's often said that the secret of successful strategy is sacrifice: knowing what we are not going to do. It's also the secret of brand strategy. Strong brands understand that in order to appeal to one customer grouping in particular they are likely to put off another customer grouping. Accepting such sacrifices lies at the heart of highly distinctive brands.

Brand management's 'dirty dozen'

Brand management today is dogged by a range of endemic operational and organizational weaknesses. Brand management should be part of the business solution. Too often, it is part of the problem.

NO HIDING PLACE

Building strong brands will never be easy. Making all the connections between buyer and seller, between brand strategy and corporate strategy, and between broad strategy and detailed day-to-day implementation, requires managers to get a vast list of things right. They have to make exactly the right product or service and offer it at the right price – and they have to generate the insight that makes this perfectly focused product and marketing possible. They have to identify exactly the right customers, talk to them, and treat them in exactly the right way, address them at the right time, through the right channel. And they have to organize internal operations, processes, and cultures to achieve all this in a seamless manner. Countless things can go wrong. And thanks to the dirty dozen pitfalls listed above, they do. Time and again.

For this reason alone, brand management needs to change. But it is being forced to change anyway. Intensifying external pressures are forcing marketers to change whether they like it or not. Slow and declining growth rates, hyper-competitive markets, overcapacity, and 'too much' customer choice mean, for example, that marketers are under intensifying pressure to deliver, and demonstrate, results. A rapidly transforming media environment is pulling the rug out from under traditional marketing communications strategies. The Internet is both upsetting traditional distribution channels and empowering consumers with greater access to information. For many such reasons, business-as-usual approaches to marketing and brand management are no longer good enough.

To rise to the occasion, we have to leave the dirty dozen behind. Strategic brand management should be a core business process demonstrating a number of characteristics. It should:

◆ be driven by consistent, objective data which can be used as a platform, rather than a substitute, for creative flow and expert judgment

◆ be backed by a common 'pivot point' of data that connects insights from different fields to enable a 'joined-up' approach to marketing

◆ enable a single, rigorous unified methodology to be used across all categories and markets

◆ act as a strategic tool influencing the value the company offers and how it creates and delivers this value

◆ unify marketers' understanding of customers, markets, and competitors

◆ create a common language that unites and informs different specialists and departments across the company internally, thereby aiding implementation.

Such a comprehensive 'joined-up' approach to brand management would inform decisions and ensure consistency from initial problem identification to execution and monitoring.

Such a 'New! Improved!' approach to brand management is indeed possible. But to make it possible, we need to start from a different place. That's what this book is about.

2 The moment of truth

Values-based brand management

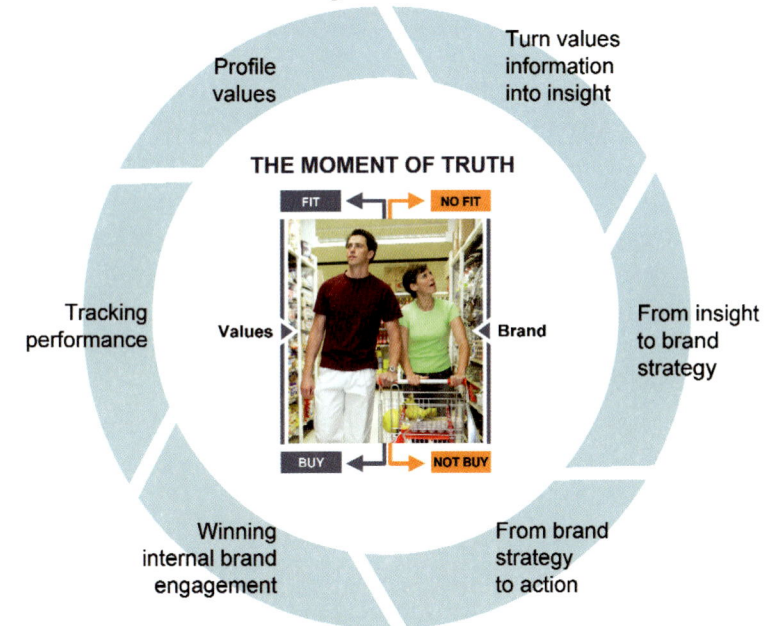

The moment of truth. For most sellers that's when a deal is clinched, a product or service is sold, and money changes hands. That's what everything else – all that work, heartache, strategy, and tactical planning – is for. To achieve that moment of truth.

But closing a sale is just a by-product of something else: the customer's belief that this choice is the right one. This belief is generated by the right alignment: when what a customer wants lines up perfectly with what the company has to offer.

So what's new?

What's new is the realization that this moment of truth is something much bigger, broader, and deeper than 'a product' that meets 'a need.' Products that meet needs are just one part of the bigger picture, where customers' 'needs' are shaped, defined, and generated by their underlying values.

This is the new and different starting point for brand management that we mentioned in Chapter 1:

> Build brands around your customers' values, *not* around the attributes of your products.

Everything in this book follows from this different starting point. The real defining moment of truth occurs when the customer feels and recognizes that his or her values are being met. It is therefore a brand manager's job to understand customers' values, and to make this understanding manifest in everything the brand does: from the finest details of the product offering, through its pricing, communication, imagery, and distribution.

This is not just an exhortation about how to do brand management. It is an *observation of fact*. If the pivotal moment of truth happens when customers recognize that their values are being addressed, actual purchases tend to reflect this recognition. This means that *the brand is defined by the values of the people who use it.*

Marketers tend to think that 'branding' is something that companies do. The marketer decides a 'brand positioning.' His or her communications agencies communicate this positioning. And hey presto! A 'brand' has been built. Don't get us wrong. These activities are absolutely necessary. But ultimately all they do is reflect the intentions of the marketers concerned. There is no guarantee that they will have the desired effect.

What actually happens in the marketplace is decided by customers. Customers buy when their values are addressed. So ultimately *customers, not marketers, define what the brand stands for.* To understand the appeal and potential of a brand, we need to understand the values of those who buy it (and the values of the people who do not buy it).

> Brands are defined by the values of the people who buy and use them.

Whether marketers like it or not, the values profile of the people who buy their brand is, effectively, the profile of their brand. It is the brand's actual impact and performance in the marketplace. To really understand a brand (and its potential future prospects), we need to understand the values of its buyers.

VALUES-BASED BRAND MANAGEMENT

Let's look at this in a little more detail. Historically, the product has been king in branding. Brands have been the packaging – the 'face' – presented to consumers to persuade them to buy the product. Branding started with what we want to sell – the offer (a product or service) – and the various devices and techniques of branding (brand name, logo design, advertising imagery and slogans, and so on) were deployed to attract the attention of the customer and present the product in the best possible light. Of course, the views of the consumer were taken into account via market research, which marketers use to tweak the product and make it more attractive. But fundamentally, the brand-building process revolved around the product.

Building brands around customers' values, on the other hand, starts not with the product but with individuals' values: the things that matter to them in their lives. Research then seeks to identify how various categories and products fit into, and serve, the customer's underlying values. Different values create different preferences. Very simply, an individual who values tranquility wants different things from an individual who values thrill and fun, for example.

Figure 2.1 illustrates the difference between the two approaches. In the first, traditional approach, branding starts with the product. Consumer research influences product details, but it is the product that defines the brand, which in turn represents these product attributes and benefits to the consumer. Under this philosophy – no matter how much lip-service brand managers give to customer focus and understanding – the product is king. And customer understanding is just one of many tools to serve the king better.

In the second approach, the brand is defined by consumers' values, and the product (and its communication) are in turn designed to reflect these values. Brands start with and are defined by the customers' values, and these values in turn define what features, price, communication,

Figure 2.1 Values-based and traditional approaches to brand management compared
Source: Roland Berger Strategy Consultants

and other attributes the product needs to develop. If all these different attributes are brought in line with the customer's values, a moment of truth happens and the customer is recruited to the brand.

Under the second approach, then, brand management starts with, and revolves around, the customer's values. The rest of this book explores what this means and how to do it. Along the way we will see how, by giving customer values the appropriate level of attention, most if not all of the brand management pitfalls we outlined in Chapter 1 can be avoided or addressed. For example, values-based brand management:

◆ Places segmentation at the heart of the brand management process, because different groups of people have different values.

♦ Is fact- and data-based, because values can be identified, researched, and analyzed in a statistically robust manner (see Chapter 3).

♦ Seamlessly integrates the rational and emotional aspects of branding because all values are both 'rational' and 'emotional' at the same time. This helps avoid many of the misunderstandings that dog modern brand management (more on this below). It also shows how brand strategy works its way back into the organization's day-to-day operations as well as its brand communications.

♦ Provides a common framework for all brand management decisions, because individuals' values are independent of different companies' industries, categories, supply chain, or product attributes.

Together these strengths – strong segmentation, integration of rational and emotional, and 'product' and 'communication,' plus a robust data-based methodology that applies regardless of product category and industry (including business-to-business) – provide a way to avoid the pitfalls of brand management's 'dirty dozen.'

WHY VALUES MATTER

So what is it about values – as opposed to product attributes or 'value' – that makes them so important? The answer is as simple as it is obvious: they are the basis upon which most people make purchasing and consumption choices. And this, of course, is what branding is all about: influencing choices.[1]

---

1 The values-based approach to brand management draws on a long history of academic research into theories of 'self-congruence': the observation that in their behaviors (including shopping and consumption), individuals seek to act in accordance with how they see themselves, how they want to see themselves, and how they want others to see them. Seminal works in self-congruence theory include E. L. Grubb and H. L. Grathwohl (1967) Consumer self-concept, symbolism, and market behavior: a theoretical approach, *Journal of Marketing*, 32, 22–27, and Joseph Sirgy (1982) Self concept in consumer behavior: a critical review, *Journal of Consumer Research*, 9 (3), 287–301.

Values are what people feel and believe is important in their lives. Individuals' personal goals and ways of life are created and shaped by their underlying values, which define what they regard as desirable and undesirable, and right and wrong. Values go deep – much deeper than either 'needs' or 'wants.' Peoples' values really do matter to them. They are personal and heartfelt. They create connections between people and the world around them. People often experience a visceral rejection of value systems that run counter to their own; they naturally gravitate towards people and things that express their own values.

Take the simple example of the motor car. The purely rational side of the motor car is that it is an efficient, convenient form of personal transport. It addresses a universal human need for personal mobility. But *how* people want to address this need – what *sort* of car they *choose* – differs in many different ways, depending on their values. Are they attracted to style or safety? Reliability or performance?

Likewise, different modes of choice express different individuals' values. Some individuals pride themselves on buying only the best, as defined by technical standards. Some always want to drive a hard bargain on price. At first sight, these seem to be highly 'rational' considerations. But that misses the real point, which is this: these particular individuals value a rational approach to life. For them, being rational is important. It is an expression of their values. However, other people with other values will prioritize other approaches. For them, perhaps, status, self-expression, or simply being different from the rest may be much more important.

Whether your mode of choice is highly rational or highly emotional, both approaches have their roots in your values. Thus, while every motor car addresses the fundamental human need of personal mobility, different people's values determine how they seek to address this need – the forms of value they are attracted to and the forms of value they are not attracted to.[2] And this is the level at which

---

2 Some people's values might lead them to reject the motor car altogether as a way of meeting their underlying need for mobility. If the environment ranks at the top of their list of concerns, for example, they might opt for greener forms of transport instead, such as the bicycle. Values therefore help to define the nature and scope of particular markets, as well as segments and offerings within these markets.

most brand choices are made, influencing both the attributes of the product (and, therefore, technologies, skills, and operations) and communications (content, media, and so on). Only by working their way backwards from the individuals' values can companies develop a coherent strategy to address all aspects of the brand management challenge in an integrated way.[3]

Figure 2.2 sums up this holistic, values-based approach to brand management. Branding starts with the individual's personal value system and how this translates into behaviors and preferences. These preferences and desires influence what the individual is 'looking for' when going to market: something that 'fits' what he or she wants. This is particularly important in an age of information overload, where individuals ruthlessly screen out messages that don't fit with their current agenda.

If the company does its job properly, it builds its core value

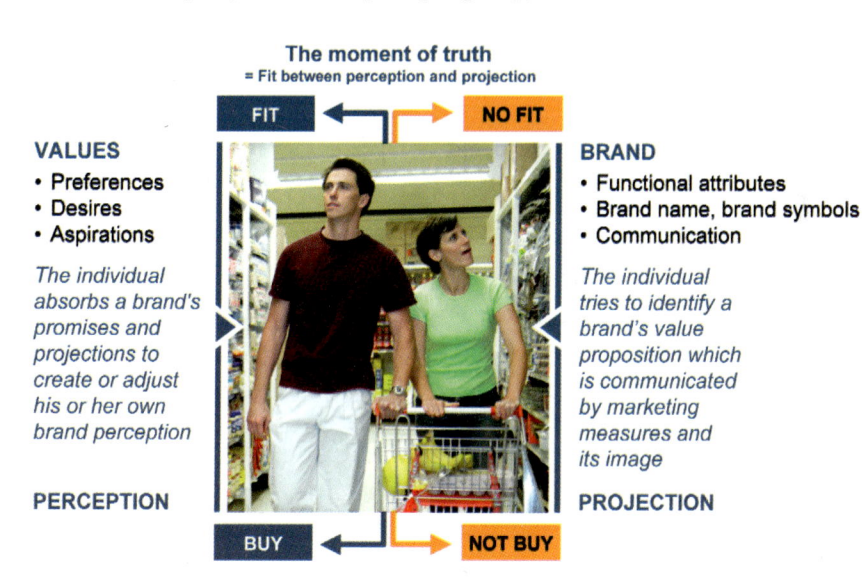

Figure 2.2 How values and brands connect
Source: Roland Berger Strategy Consultants

_____

3 The above example is, of course, highly simplified. In real life, most people want different combinations of things: style and reliability, performance and value for money, and so on: it is different bundles of values that define us as individuals. People who are attracted to similar bundles create different customer groupings or segments (see Chapter 3).

proposition – its brand – around these values, and the brand's values are then expressed in everything it does: its functional attributes, what it communicates, how it communicates, which channels it uses, and so on. If there is a fit between what the buyer sees (not only the brand's marketing communications, but every 'touch point' or source of information, including previous experience, other users of the brand, and so on), that crucial moment of truth takes place. The customer is now much more likely to buy. If there is a disconnect, the willingness to purchase declines.

Seeing the brand management process in this way creates a series of 'pinch points.' In particular:

◆ Do we understand the individual's or group's values?

◆ Have we aligned the brand's value proposition – across everything it does – to these values?

◆ Are we communicating this proposition in such a way that individuals or groups see these values as their own?

These pinch points apply to all forms of brand: product and service brands, ingredient and corporate or umbrella brands, even (as we'll see later in more detail) to business-to-business brands.

Indeed, as we'll see later, the values-based approach to brand management becomes all the more important as we move beyond traditional branding heartlands in packaged goods to industries with multiple customer touch points such as retail, telecommunications, utilities, and fashion.

Values apply as much to businesses as they do individuals

For example, some businesses value qualities such as integrity and commitment, while others value qualities such as durability and excellence, while yet others value creativity and innovation or (of course) straightforward price competitiveness.

A values-based approach to brand management can deliver some hugely important benefits. Below we list some of them. Over the coming chapters we aim to show how, and why, these benefits naturally emerge from a values-based approach.

A universal methodology

Customer values are independent from the minutiae and details of any and every particular industry, category, supply chain, product, or service. Starting with values therefore provides an 'anchor' or thread uniting the company's marketing approach, depending on the market or category it is working within.

Strategy, consistency, and momentum

Unlike markets, customer values are very slow to change. Values change over generations, and an individual's values may change over the course of a lifetime. But they do not change minute to minute or hour to hour. In many marketing departments, the urgent continually drives out the important: tactical, short-term initiatives and responses dominate marketers' time and attention; strategic considerations fall by the wayside. An underlying focus on slow-changing values provides the company with an ongoing, steadying strategic perspective. Focusing on values, then, helps marketers build the consistency and momentum that are hallmarks of all great brands. If the brand is designed to appeal to a certain core set of consumer values, for example, it's virtually unthinkable that the brand's underlying strategy will be changed overnight just because a new marketing director has taken over.

Of course, marketers need to work with tactics as well. But they now have a litmus test by which to judge every individual initiative: does it help or hinder us in our quest to appeal to, and serve, this particular values grouping? In this way, instead of disrupting strategic momentum through continually chopping and changing, each separate 'tactical' initiative can be used to help build momentum and express consistency. Putting consumer values at the heart of the brand gives marketers a clear and consistent set of guidelines to help them create synergy between disparate activities and build momentum over time.

Fact and data-based

Values are open to – indeed encourage – a fact-driven, data-based approach to brand strategy. One of the drawbacks of traditional approaches to marketing is endemic communication breakdowns between 'creatives,' who focus on communications and the emotional side of things, and operations people who focus on products, processes, and objective facts. The different styles, modes, and interests of these different groups create different languages and priorities.

Defining a brand's profile in terms of the people who buy it gives marketers no room to argue the toss. The facts about who buys (and doesn't buy) an existing brand can be ascertained by market research. And this provides a central reference point for all subsequent research and analysis. From now on, every additional piece of data – such as income, profession and other socio-demographic status, lifestyle, media consumption habits, shopping habits, product and brand preferences – can be linked to this core values information. Instead of dealing with many incommensurate and unconnected data sets (such as, how does media consumption link into choice of shopping channel and brand?), we now have a common foundation which makes it possible to connect and relate all this data. We can, for instance, build a sound, data-based understanding of the spending power, behaviors, and preferences of each values segment. This 'joined up' data is key to identifying not only the existence of different market opportunities but also their relative financial attractiveness.

Fresh insights

Researching and understanding brands first and foremost by the values of the people who buy (and don't buy) them almost invariably opens up new territories to explore. What are the main values of different customer groupings? How do they differ? How are they similar? Are all these values groupings being addressed by existing brands, or is there a gap in the market? How do these values translate into potentially different value propositions and communications strategies?

Values-based research broadens marketers' perspective, helping them to understand the dynamics of entire markets. For example,

> ## Table 2.1 Strengths of values-based brand management
>
> ◆ A universal methodology
>
> ◆ A strategic perspective, providing consistency and momentum
>
> ◆ Fact and data-based decision making
>
> ◆ Insight generating
>
> ◆ Aids effective implementation
>
> ◆ Creates a common language
>
> ◆ Facilitates a global view
>
> ◆ Generates a healthy dose of humility

companies taking such an approach have understood why some brands are losing momentum (by failing to evolve with their customers' value sets), how they have missed complete market opportunities (because some value sets are not being served by any existing player), and how, in some markets, values tend to move in one direction but brands in another.

A common language

Values-based research helps create the sort of robust, joined-up market data that helps everyone in the company – CEOs and finance directors as well as marketers – to understand the size and scope of different marketing options and their potential rewards: it creates a common language which unites the entire company around profitably meeting its customers' needs.

Aids implementation

The clarity of focus created by the values-based approach, backed by robust data and a common language, makes effective detailed day-to-day implementation of brand strategies much easier. It also helps brand managers manage agency relationships. Too many brilliant strategies die because of poor implementation. Values-based analysis provides the backbone needed to avoid this pitfall.

A global perspective

Values are basically the same the world over because they express what's common to human beings around the world. The degree to which certain value sets are adhered to varies, as does the relative proportion of people with different values. The permutations and combinations might vary too. But fundamentally, you can find the same values wherever you are in the world. Working on the basis of values (as opposed to highly specific market characteristics) allows marketers to see what unites markets, to develop tools that are applicable across different geographical markets, and to obtain insights that support the building of international and global brands.

A holistic view of the brand

A common mistaken assumption about brands is that they are constructed from two essentially separate components: 'the product' which addresses functional, rational needs and 'the communication' which generates emotional associations. In reality (as we'll see below) every product generates emotional responses, and communication has a rational, functional role too. Both should be united by the fact that they reflect and address the individual's values. Understanding values, and how they are made manifest in both products and communications, provides us with the integrating, unifying perspective we need to manage brands effectively.

A healthy dose of humility

The product-first approach to branding leads marketers to define brands in terms of product attributes – which are, in turn, created by marketers. When product-based brand managers manage their brands, they have a nasty habit of gazing admiringly into a mirror of their own creation. The values-based approach teaches us that brands are not defined by marketers working in an ivory tower somewhere: brands are defined by the people who use them. How well a brand performs depends on who actually buys it. Values-based brand strategies don't allow marketers the luxury of flights of fancy.

NAVIGATING THE MARKETING MAZE

In Greek mythology, King Minos of Crete built a labyrinth so complex that no one entering it could ever find his or her way out again. The labyrinth was stalked by a terrible beast, the Minotaur, who continually demanded sacrifices in the form of human flesh: young men and women of Athens.

One of these Athenians, Theseus, volunteered to enter the labyrinth to kill the Minotaur. Ariadne, King Minos's daughter, fell in love with Theseus. She gave him a piece of thread which he unwound as he traveled through the labyrinth, and this enabled him to kill the Minotaur, retrace his steps, and find his way out.

To complete his journey safely, Theseus had to avoid countless wrong turnings, which were all too easy to make in the murky darkness of the labyrinth, but extremely dangerous nevertheless. In Chapter 1 we discussed the 'dirty dozen' pitfalls of brand management. All of these wrong turnings relate to the implementation and execution of brand strategies. But they are intimately connected to another set of wrong turnings which are equally dangerous: myths and misunderstandings about what brands do and how.

Clasping our understanding firmly as an Ariadne-thread to guide us through the marketing maze, let's quickly review these dangerous misunderstandings to see how values-based brand management helps avoid them.

Misunderstanding 1: 'Brands create differentiation'

It is often claimed that in a world of increasing product parity, 'branding' is the secret of success because it adds an extra layer of differentiation 'on top' of the mere product. This theory turns the essence of brand management on its head. Strong brands express a high degree of alignment to different groups of customers who have different values. Differentiation is not invented or added by brand managers. Its real source is the people whose values the brand addresses. Different people are, quite simply, different, and real brand differentiation comes from understanding these differences and reflecting them back to the customer via the forms and types of value brands offer. It is the *process* of brand management, not the superficial activities of 'branding,' that delivers real differentiation.

The theory that 'branding' can somehow create differentiation out of thin air actually turns the win–win heart of brand management – the aligning moment of truth – into a tissue of lies. The job of brands is to express real differentness. If branding degenerates into a cynical attempt to hide sameness, the brand will cease to be a source of real value for either side.

The mythology of branding

How brands add value to buyers and sellers alike is widely misunderstood, with damaging consequences, as the examples outlined in this section show.

Too many companies think that branding is all about communication – and an easy way to boost margins. As a result, many consumers see branding as little more than a 'con.'

Brands create value by facilitating moments of truth – when customer values and company value propositions align. These moments of truth are the 'on' switch of wealth-creating activity.

Misunderstanding 2: 'Brands deliver superior margins'

Warming to the 'product parity' theme, many marketers argue that in a world where most products are pretty similar, it is 'branding' that makes them seem different, and it is this 'branding' ('differentness' communicated via advertising, design, logos, and so on) that persuades customers to pay more.

Again, this is a mirror image of the reality. Superior margins are a by-product of superior value. And superior value comes from moments of truth; from the brand's ability to truly address customers' values in the richest, deepest way possible. Only by aligning their total value offering to customer values – the moment of truth – will firms be able to generate superior margins.

Misunderstanding 3: 'Branding is the soft, emotional, fluffy stuff'

Many marketing theories create an unbridgeable divide between 'the product,' which is seen as a rational, functional thing addressing rational, functional 'needs,' and 'the communication,' which is emotional. Products are created by rational people working in rational ways in factories. And communications are created by emotional, creative types working in emotional, creative advertising agencies.

The reality is that it is customers who bring emotions to the party. A mundane task such as cleaning the toilet, for example, can and does trigger all sorts of powerful emotions. These emotions may revolve around a sense of orderliness and control. They may refer to the pride and satisfaction of 'being a good mother.' Or they may relate to negative emotions such as disgust or the boredom of daily chores. Which emotions become dominant is a reflection of the individual's overall values. Whatever the emotion, however, it is not 'created' by advertising agencies via advertisements. It is created naturally by individuals in the course of their everyday lives.

Effective brands don't 'add' emotional attributes to emotion-less things. They recognize that the emotions people bring to their everyday lives reflect their underlying values, and they seek to address these underlying values and associated emotions through every touch point in a seamless, holistic way.

Misunderstanding 4: 'Brands are instruments of market control'

Marketers often describe their goals in terms of changing something about the consumer: changing attitudes, perceptions, behaviors. Marketers often see themselves as deploying different elements of the marketing mix to achieve these ends. Marketing becomes a quest for customer control.

Price promotions, for example, change customer behaviors in desirable ways by prompting the customer to buy more, or to buy the item being promoted instead of a full-price competitor. Likewise, by inserting the right messages and associations into the customer's head, marketers hope that 'branding' will change customer attitudes and preferences in favor of their product.

Once again, this confuses appearance with the reality. Marketers seem to be 'in control' of markets when their brands are perfectly aligned to customers' needs and values: when those pivotal moments of truth are frequent and plentiful. The *appearance* of market control is a by-product of excellent alignment. Marketers who see brand management in terms of somehow controlling customer attitudes and preferences ultimately attempt to turn their brands into instruments of manipulation, thereby destroying the win–win heart of branding.

They might as well not bother. Aligning brands to customer values breeds moments of truth, and superior margins can follow. Attempting to align customers to brands (on the other hand) is both expensive and futile.

Misunderstanding 5: 'Brands are mechanisms of push'

The origins of branding lie in companies' attempts to present their products to the buying public in the best possible light. The purpose of the paraphernalia of brand communications – packaging designs and logos, advertising slogans and imagery, jingles, slogans, and so on – was to draw consumers' attention to the product and persuade them to buy.

Communicating the benefits of products to customers is an essential part of the brand management process. But it only works if the benefits that are being communicated fit with what the customer is looking for. We are back to moments of truth again. The essence of good brand management lies in 'pull' not 'push.' It lies in the company's ability to *internalize* and reflect customers' values so that these customers are drawn to what the company offers. It does not lie in the mechanics of externally pushing products and messages at customers.

A quick look at the above misunderstandings shows how closely connected they are to the dirty dozen pitfalls we discussed in Chapter 1.

Each one of the myths described above creates its own disconnect: between 'product' and 'communication'; between 'rational' and 'emotional'; between operations and the marketing department; between the company's interests and the customer's interests. Silo-itis, a failure to speak a common language, to develop accountable processes, to identify valid measures: all these flaws are inevitable as soon as the myths begin to take hold.

We need the Ariadne-thread of values-based brand management – our understanding of the moment of truth – to navigate our way round both the theoretical misunderstandings and the practical pitfalls that dog brand management today.

SUMMARY

In this chapter we suggest that starting the process of brand management at a different place – with the values of the people who buy the brand – provides the unifying, integrating thread we need to navigate today's marketing maze.

A values-based approach to brand management has huge advantages. It is fact-based and data-driven. It focuses on market fundamentals, helping to create fresh insights that can open up new strategic directions. It provides companies with a common language which helps them identify, explain, and implement marketing strategies. It provides a foundation for momentum-building consistency; provides the information needed to choose between alternative marketing and brand strategies; and offers a common methodology that works equally well across different industries, categories, and geographies.

Looking forward, we shall see how a values-based approach to brand strategy provides us with the Ariadne-thread that enables us to tackle all the key challenges and phases of the brand management process. These include:

◆ strategy formulation (including post-merger marketing strategies)

◆ deciding on new product and service priorities

◆ changing brand architectures and brand portfolios

- ◆ segmentation and targeting

- ◆ positioning

- ◆ internal and employee branding

- ◆ determining the optimum marketing mix

- ◆ effectiveness tracking

- ◆ reviewing the organization of marketing.

But first we need to answer some basic questions. What *are* people's values? And how can we discover and understand them?

3   Profiling consumer values

Values-based brand management

Dr Karl Bergmann is a 47-year-old lawyer who works for an internationally renowned law firm. He and his family live in Grünwald, one of Munich's most coveted suburbs. As a lawyer, he is well established in his field and regularly publishes commentaries in a German judicial magazine.

Karl Bergmann has strong principles and values and leads a goal-oriented life. He always carefully plans his days and does not like any deviations from his detailed agenda.

Karl's oldest son Jan leads his life differently. To Karl, he seems careless and lacking in concrete professional objectives. While Jan is satisfied with his lack of direction, his father finds it perplexing. Karl would give anything to make Jan realize that seriousness and a commitment to one's studies are a prerequisite for future success.

Figure 3.1 Dr Karl Bergmann and some of his favorite objects

Jan, 21, studies business administration at the University of Cologne, where he shares an apartment with two fellow students.

At the moment Jan does not have a girlfriend, as he feels too young to be in a serious relationship. He enjoys living life to its fullest, and avoids any kind of commitment. In his spare time he plays soccer, enjoys snowboarding and spends a lot of time playing video games.

Jan goes out every evening to meet his friends in bars and 'see and be seen.' He thinks of himself as a trendsetter and thrives on impressing others. Jan is strongly attached to his gadgets and is addicted to his mobile phone. Jan's motto is best described as 'live every day like it's your last, without any regrets.'

Figure 3.2 Jan and some of his favorite objects

Jan and Dr Karl Bergmann are very different, and if we picked through their brand and product preferences and priorities we might be able to identify some of these differences. Karl Bergmann is attracted towards things with proven quality, for example. He admires and values new technology, and he looks for (and gets) good service. He is not price sensitive: he expects to pay more to get more. He also has a strong antipathy to what he regards as irresponsible and reckless thrill-seeking – hence his disagreements with his son.

Jan has one thing in common with Karl: he too likes new technology. But that's where the similarities end. Jan's attraction is to everything new and cool, to every new experience. This would drive Karl up the wall. Jan's bargain hunting leaves Karl cold. Jan's carefree, passionate nature clashes with Karl's sober rationality.

Also, being a thinking, socially responsible citizen, Karl is concerned about the environment and thinks 'fairness' is important to a civilized society. Jan has no such scruples. He is far too focused on living for the moment to worry about such things. In fact, when he comes across people who express such concerns it positively irritates him.

We could go on drawing such verbal – and visual – pictures of different people forever. But is it possible to capture the essence of such similarities and differences in a standardized way? The answer is yes. Every individual's basic values can be mapped in a chart that sums up his or her tendency to agree or disagree with values that are common to people the world over. In Europe our research has identified 19 core values that are common – in varying degrees and combinations – to the population. These 19 values are summed up in Table 3.1. We will describe these values, and how they have been identified, in more detail below. But first, let's look at a useful way of visualizing them.

Figure 3.3 shows how Karl Bergmann and Jan show up when charted against these common consumer values. Blue areas indicate values the individual is specifically drawn towards, and the contour lines show how strongly. The more contour lines there are, the more the individual is drawn towards that particular value. Red areas indicate the values that positively turn the person off. Again, the more contour lines there are, the stronger the tendency. White areas indicate areas where the individual is no different from the rest of the population. In this way, what was a highly impressionistic and qualitative depiction of a particular individual's personality can be visualized and mapped.

Table 3.1 The 19 core values of consumers in Europe

Quality	Classic
Proven	New and cool
Service	Thrill and fun
Personal efficiency	Passion
24/7 pro-tech	Tranquil
Customized	Purism
Clanning	Nature
Carefree	Fair
Vitality	Smart shopping
Total cost	

VALUES PROFILING: THE METHODOLOGY

But how do we create such maps? Each map is based on each individual's answers to a series of carefully crafted questions, designed to tease out his or her attraction to, or repulsion from, the values in question. Each value is addressed by a number of different questions, and the contour lines are calculated from the individual's answers to the complete range.

Mathematically speaking, every answer to each question either builds a 'hill' (blue for positive) or etches a 'valley' (red for negative). But a three-dimensional values 'landscape' isn't as easy to understand as a simple two-dimensional chart, where the valleys are marked red and the hills are marked blue.

The resulting data can be aggregated to create profiles of the users of a particular brand, the participants in a market, the viewers of a

Dr Karl Bergmann

Jan

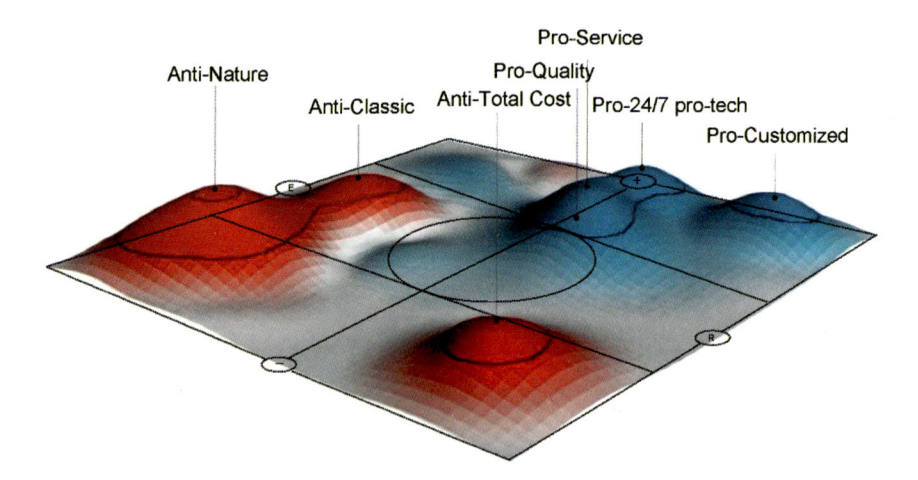

Figure 3.3 Dr Karl Bergmann's and Jan's value profiles
Source: Roland Berger Strategy Consultants, TNS data (Germany, March 2002, n=1500, population 14–65 years, CATI)

Figure 3.4 Calculating a value profile's contours
Source: Roland Berger Strategy Consultants, TNS data (Germany, March 2002, n=1500, population 14–65 years, CATI)

particular television show, the residents of a particular street .... In fact, once the core research has been done, the data can be sliced and diced to focus on any aspect of reality researchers want to investigate.

They can look at how the values of one income group differ from another, or at value differences between regions or age groups. They can even map entire markets to identify which values competing brands are serving best – and where the gaps in the market are.

But how do we know these are the values that really matter? Why not 15 values? Or 23? And how can we be confident that the data is robust?

The roots of this values-based approach to brand analysis lie in a decision by a consortium of leading European packaged goods manufacturers and retailers to investigate the drivers of 'consumer enthusiasm.' The consortium, called Efficient Consumer Response Europe (or ECR Europe for short), asked Roland Berger Strategy Consultants to identify things the industry as whole could do to address a series of pressing problems.

These problems are familiar to anyone working in the industry. 'We want to stop fighting over who gets what sized piece of the cake: we need to grow the cake.' 'Overall, the grocery industry's share of wallet is falling as consumers decide to spend more of their disposable income on other things. Is there anything we can do to reverse the trend?'

A cross-industry working group, including representatives from leading manufacturers and retailers such as Albert Heijn and Tesco, Procter & Gamble and Kellogg, decided to look outside their back yard to 'best in class' companies in different industry sectors across the world: companies such as Yahoo, Hennes & Mauritz in fashion retailing, Dell, and Nike. What is it that makes them special? Are there learnings that could be transferred?

At this stage the aim was simply to look at what seemed to work and to identify common factors, including the underlying consumer trends these successful companies seemed to be responding to. Having studied the experience of these best-in-class operators, the working group came to a simple but profound conclusion. Each outstanding company focuses hard on addressing a very specific group of values. Often these values are very different, even contradictory, and the trick is to address them simultaneously. By the way, this also means the companies deliberately do not try to address certain other values at the same time.

Take Hennes & Mauritz, for example. Its success is founded on its ability to offer young consumers the thrill and fun of catwalk-style fashion at prices they can afford. Thrill and fun. Low cost. These are not just *product* attributes, the working group realized. They are *values* this particular consumer group are particularly drawn towards; and Hennes & Mauritz has become expert at addressing them through the items of clothing it carries, its shops – indeed, its entire business model. Hennes & Mauritz is a success because it really understands, and addresses, its target customers' *values*. That is *how* it delivers them *value*.

Up to this stage, however, all the working group had was an interesting but unsubstantiated hypothesis. True, the hypothesis was drawn from the insights of some of the world's most experienced marketers. But still, it was only a hypothesis. The next step was validation: a massive research project which simply asked consumers open-ended questions about what mattered to them, in aspects of their lives related to consumption.

In many ways, this was the opposite of traditional market research. Most market research focuses very tightly on a specific set of questions, to which companies want specific answers. In most market research, the agenda has already been decided and the resulting outcome is therefore necessarily fixed and limited. In contrast, this research had no preconceptions. No agenda. Its purpose was not to pursue the particular agenda of any particular company. Its purpose was to discover the consumers' agenda.

The end result was a bank of around 2000 statements about what motivates or demotivates people, derived from open-ended questions and discussions with consumers. The researchers used factor analysis to create clusters from a vast database (200 answers each from approximately 2000 people means 400,000 separate data points). They then analyzed the correlations, looking for those statements that appeared wholly redundant (that is, they were effectively covered by another statement), or that generated ambiguous or hard-to-interpret results. In this way, by analyzing and reanalyzing, the original bank of 2000 statements was boiled down to a battery of around 80 statements. These 80 statements effectively sum up the values that individuals say matter to them.

The next step was to understand how answers to different statements tended to cluster. With each statement being given a value of 0–4, which statements tend to be answered in a similar way? Table 3.2 shows some sample statements identified by the research as indicative of individuals' underlying values. Those that tend to cluster define a 'value,' and the combination of values adhered to or rejected by the individual creates that individual's 'value signature' (as we saw with Karl Bergmann and Jan).

All in all the research identified 19 values that are common to most consumer markets. A battery of around 80 attitudinal questions was developed to identify which consumers adopt which values. What are these values? Table 3.1 outlined them. In Table 3.3 they are given in a little more detail.

Since then, the research has been extended and deepened to cover 70,000 consumers in 16 countries including Germany, the United Kingdom, Brazil, Mexico, China, and Japan. The same methodology

Table 3.2 Examples of core values statements identified in original research

Tranquil
I am most annoyed by hectic and busy environments.

Purism
It annoys me that goods are so disposable.

Nature
I prefer products containing few pollutants and produced using environmentally friendly methods.

Fair
The government needs to do more to protect the rights of the consumer.

Clanning
The best experiences are those you have with friends or family.

Carefree
I often do things on the spur of the moment.

Thrill and fun
I don't want to think about the future, I live for the here and now.

has been applied to business-to-business markets (15 core values have been identified in these markets, down from 22 candidate values identified in the original open-ended research). And the same research methodology has been extended across geographical regions, always using the same painstaking 'bottom-up' approach. That is why, for example, the final battery of questions used in research in China and Japan differs from those used, say, in Germany.

In China, for example, the original open-ended research revealed one common value that hardly appears on the European radar screen. We call this value 'aspiration,' reflecting the large number of Chinese individuals for whom rising out of their current social status is a critical driver in their lives. Japan has an extra value too, but it is very different. It reflects an almost obsessive 'shop till you drop' attitude amongst some Japanese consumers. Thus, as noted in Chapter 2, while most consumer values are the same around the world (even though they are embraced to different degrees by different proportions of the population), they are not exactly the same. For values profiling, both the similarities and the differences need to be identified and understood.

This methodology has since been applied, refined, and tested in more than 100 major projects across the world, in a wide range of categories including automotive, chemicals/oil, FMCG, financial services, tourism, hotels, pharmaceuticals and medical technologies, retail, telecommunications, utilities, and fashion.

DEVELOPING VALUE PROFILES

It is one thing to identify the most common and dearly held values, but what about the maps of Karl Bergmann and Jan as shown in Figure 3.3? Why are the various values scattered around the square like that? And what is the real significance of those contour lines?

The placing of values is not random. It is derived mathematically (see Appendix for more technical details). To achieve this visual map, we test out mathematically (using multi-dimensional scaling) how 'close' each value is to all the other values. Values that tend to be held in common are placed on a grid relatively close together, while values that are seen as opposites are placed far away from each other. Thus as Figure 3.5 illustrates, the values Fair and Nature tend to go together, while the value Thrill and fun is as far away from Total cost as it could be.

Table 3.3 The 19 core consumer values,

Fair
Need for high ethical standards; rejection of exploitation; solidarity, active social engagement; readiness for self-sacrifice and rebellion on behalf of humanity

Passion
Need for admiration, reassurance; attention seeking, expressive attitudes; living out profound emotion, enthusiasm; showing off, narcissism, eroticism

Nature
Need for high ecological standards, holistic views; trusting, in harmony with and protective of nature, taking care of animals; giving up own needs for nature

Classic
Need for timeless elegance and style; beauty, aesthetics and design; conservative hedonism; conservative status and elitist thinking

Purism
Need for reduction to the essentials and simplicity, pure things, minimalism; understatement; not wasting things, rejection of affluence, looking for long-lasting things

Tranquil
Need for calmness, peace, relaxation; slowing down, de-stressing, regeneration; looking for harmony, inner peace, avoiding stress and a hectic life; soft escapism

Smart shopping
Need for systematic seeking of 'value for money'; active bargain hunting; clever attitude; price sensitive; skepticism about a brand's pricing

Quality
Need for objective measurable performance criteria; effectiveness, durability, reliability; high and continuous supplier effort; order; cleanliness

Total cost
Need for systematic least-cost purchase; extreme penny-pinching; extreme minimalism. Also rebelling against materialistic society.

Proven
Need for successful experience; maximum security, reliability; authority, scientific proof; tradition, routine, 'the good old things'; extreme discipline, perfectionism

Vitality
Need for physical and mental fitness; activity, vitality; health orientation, healthy living. Also liveliness, mobility, independence, initiative.

Thrill and fun
Need to have 'adrenalin in the blood'; thrill, risk and adventure seeking; rebellious rule breaking; extreme challenge, pushing the limits; self-definition

Clanning
Need to belong, warmth, friendship, team spirit; desire for acceptance in a group; spending time with friends or family; having a 'good time' together

Carefree
Need for light heartedness; easygoing, optimistic, positive; spontaneity, playful diversity; 'Hakuna Matata' – no worries

Service
Need for uncomplicated information and fulfillment; for competent and practical advice; for sensitivity, respect, and honesty; for 'warm' interaction

New and cool
Need to set trends, rule breaking; maximum variety and stimuli; avant-gardist status and elitist thinking; self-differentiation from the 'gray masses'

24/7 pro-tech
Need for application of newest/latest technology; scientific innovation; fast information and access, anytime, anywhere; 'cold' transaction

Personal efficiency
Need to make the best out of time; individual time management; extreme efficiency, best possible performance; speed; expecting stand-by solutions

Customized
Need for maximum individuality; just-for-me availability; direct involvement, one-to-one; controllable uniqueness, exclusivity; maximum flexibility and variety

The same analysis puts the most commonly held values – values that are embraced by more of the population as opposed to values with minority appeal – closer to the center (marked by the circle). Thus the most common values tend to be those of Service, Quality, Price, and 'Clanning' (or 'Being a part of'), while Thrill and fun, Customized, Total cost, and Fair are minority values. The result is a simple two-dimensional grid depicting each value at a mathematically derived 'distance' from every other value.

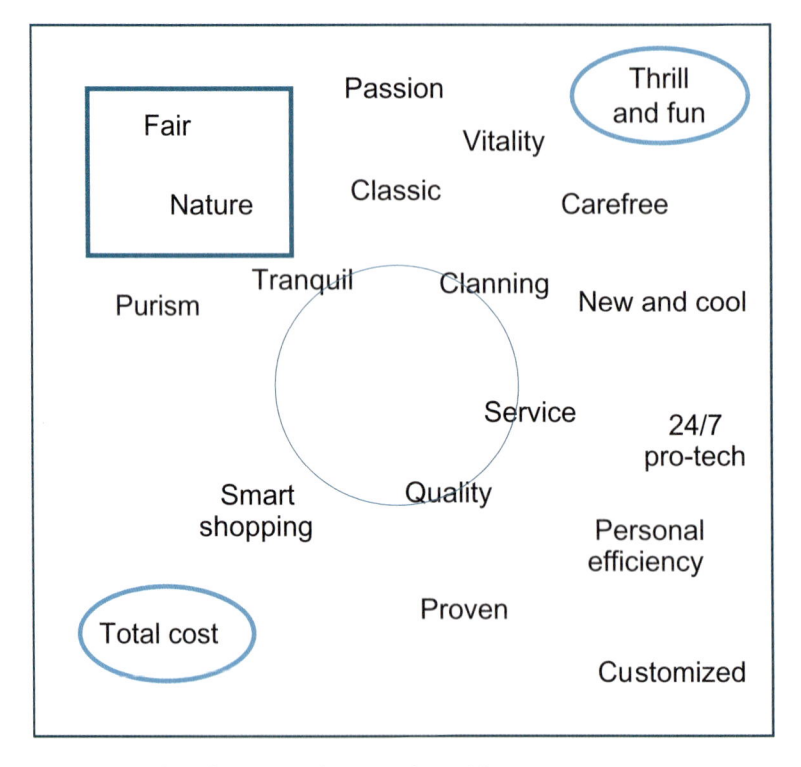

Figure 3.5 Mapping the core values on the grid
Source: Roland Berger Strategy Consultants

Once this grid has been created, there are further ways of using it. For example, Figure 3.6 shows the overall tendencies of people whose values tend to cluster in each of the four main quadrants of the grid. The top-left quadrant is inhabited by people for whom ethics and responsibility are important; the top right by people who value fun and pleasurable experiences, for example. Also, as we can see, the map also represents a continuum along two dimensions. The 'northern' dimensions tend towards a highly emotional approach to value; the southern end depicts more rational values. The west–east axis represents relative degrees of willingness to spend money.

Drilling down in slightly more detail, we can identify smaller, more particular regions of the map, each with more closely related values (see Figure 3.7). We have invented a series of names to describe them, distinguishing between a general tendency towards 'hedonism' as opposed to 'performance,' and between different 'styles' such as 'traditional' and 'progressive.' Some values span the borders of this six-part grid, meaning that they are ingredients of two parts of the grid.

Summed up, these more detailed values groups are:

◆ Altruism: Fair, Nature, and Purism.

◆ Traditional hedonism: Passion, Vitality, Classic, Tranquil, and Clanning.

◆ Progressive hedonism: Thrill and fun, Carefree, New and cool.

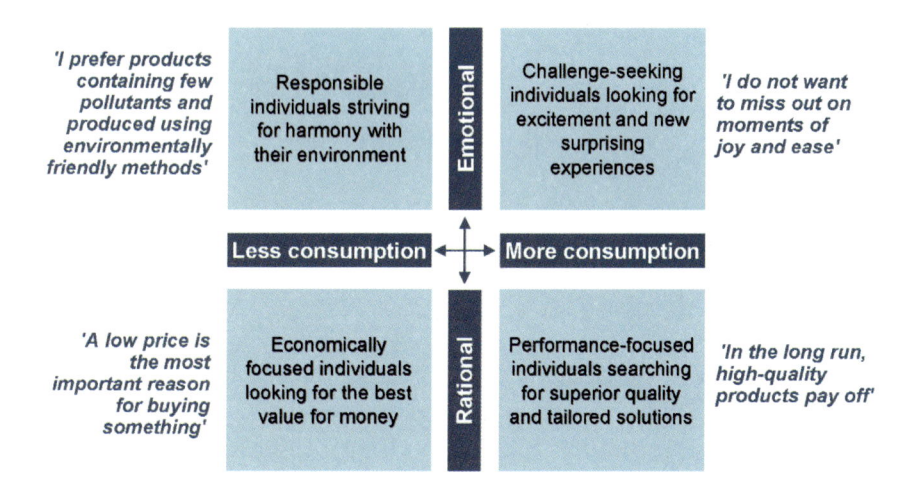

Figure 3.6 Different quadrants in a values profile
Source: Roland Berger Strategy Consultants

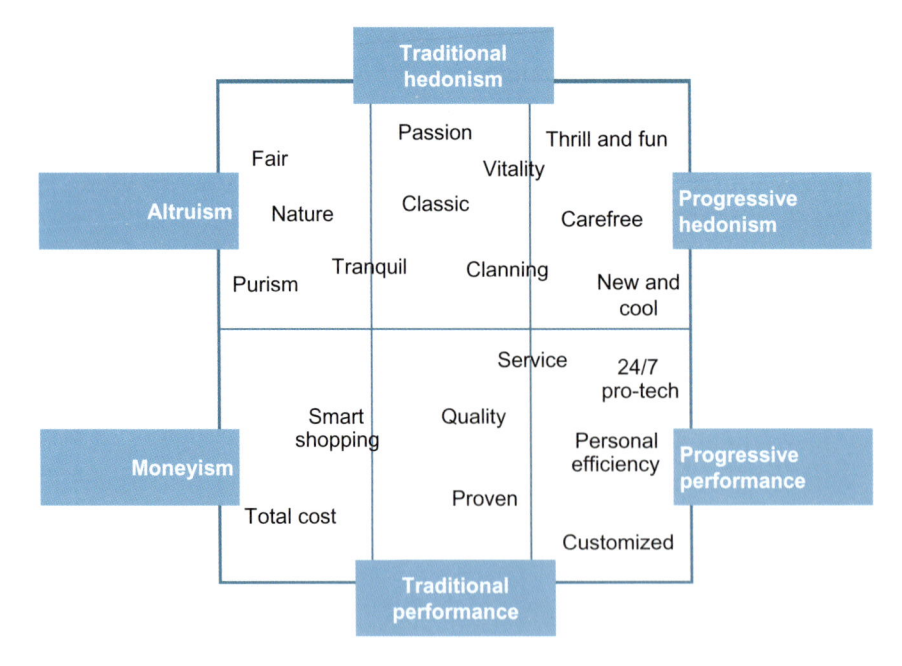

Figure 3.7 Different regions of the values grid
Source: Roland Berger Strategy Consultants

♦ Progressive performance: 24/7 pro-tech, Personal efficiency, Customized.

♦ Traditional performance: Service, Quality, Proven, and Smart shopping.

♦ Moneyism: Smart shopping and Total cost.

No individual's values will ever sit perfectly in just one region of the grid. As we'll see below when we discuss values archetypes, it is the patterns and combinations that make people so different and so fascinating.

If we look back to Figure 3.3 on page 33 for example, we can see that Karl Bergmann rejects progressive hedonist values and lives mainly in the 'performance' regions, both traditional and progressive, with a tinge of altruism. Jan, on the other hand, lives in regions of progressive hedonism and performance, with a tinge of moneyism. He is also a complete rejector of altruist values.

Finally, one more point about the contour lines. As we've seen, contour lines represent degrees of statistical significance. A contour line shows how different this individual or group is *from the average of the total sample*. This is a crucial point which underlines any correct interpretation of values profiles. A 'blue' or 'red' region – relative attraction or repulsion – *is indeed relative*: relative to the average of the relevant sample. Every values profile depicts one particular individual or group *compared with* another group. In the case of Karl Bergmann and Jan, for example, the sample in question was 16–65-year-old German citizens. *Change the sample, and you change the contour lines.*

A word on terminology

To help us talk about clusters of values, we have used terms such as 'hedonism,' 'performance,' 'progressive,' and 'traditional.' Later, when we discuss archetypes, we also select names to describe groups of people whose values cluster similarly. These names can sometimes look like horrible jargon. They are simply designed as a shorthand way of describing specific clusters of values. The important thing is the cluster of values, not the name.

Also, these names are meant to be purely descriptive. There is no value judgment intended when we say one person is a 'hedonist' or another person an 'altruist.' They are simply terms designed to describe clusters of values that are common across populations of people.

To really understand the significance of any profile – those contour lines – we need to pay attention to the subject and the sample it is being compared to. This becomes critical when researching niches and segments. If you want to understand the profile of a luxury car brand like Mercedes or BMW, for example, comparing it with the sample 'all car users' is unlikely to reveal a useful map. If the sample is 'luxury car buyers,' however, then the differences between the brand profiles become much sharper.

AGGREGATING PROFILES

Once an individual's value profile has been assembled it can be used as a building block for any and all sorts of different analysis. Think of any attribute you like. As long as this data has been collected and is attributable to the individual concerned, then the link can be established – and averages can be calculated across complete samples or populations. In this way, we can identify the values of any chosen slice, be it defined by age, income, market participation, brand loyalty, whatever.

> All the value profiles show *relative*, not absolute levels of commitment. A contour line shows that this individual (or group) is more inclined (or averse) to this particular value than the average of the sample the individual is being compared with. *Every chart depicts variation from the sample average*, so every chart highlights visually what makes the individual special or different, compared with a specific population.

The principle is illustrated by Figure 3.8, which contrasts the values of different German age cohorts: 16–29-year-olds versus 40–49-year-olds. The contrast is marked. Compared with the rest of the population (remember, every contour line represents a statistical deviation from the average), young Germans are positively rejecting values associated with Nature and Fair, as well as Quality and Service, while they are particularly attracted to the values that cluster around Carefree and Passion. The profile of 40–49-year-olds is almost the exact opposite, positively embracing Nature, Fair, and Tranquil on the one hand, and Service, Quality, and Smart shopping on the other. Carefree, Vitality, and Passion are positive turn-offs.

The implications for brands are clear. Brands that 'tune in' to the values of one age group are unlikely to appeal to the other age group. Indeed, the research from which these figures are drawn shows that when it comes to values, only 7 percent of brands in Germany fit well

16–29 years   **40–49 years**

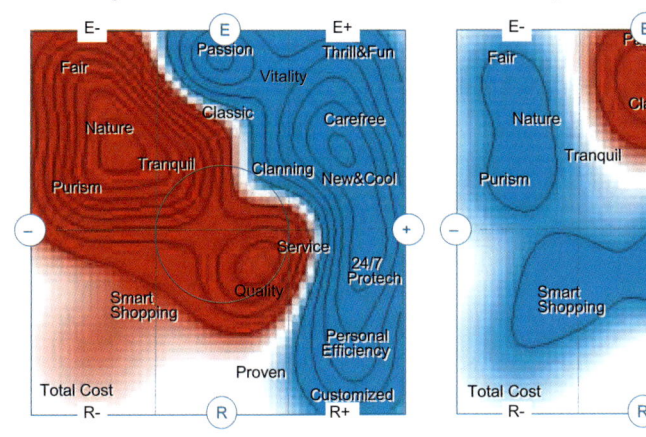

Figure 3.8 How different age groups' values differ
Source: Roland Berger Strategy Consultants, Roland Berger Market Research data
(Germany, March 2005, n=2004, population 16–69 years, CATI)

with the values of those over 60, while a third of all brands have values profiles that fit the younger age groups. Considering the 'baby boomer' demographic bulge now affecting Germany (and many other countries), this suggests there are major opportunities for brands that find ways of appealing to the values of the over-60s.

Figure 3.8 is just one example of an endless variety of possible analyses. These different forms of analysis can be used to build and implement brand strategies, as is shown in the next chapter.

But first, let us explore one particularly useful way of slicing and dicing the core data: via values archetypes.

ARCHETYPES (EXAMPLES)

Archetypes are created by clustering groups of people with similar values. Archetypes are constructed mathematically 'bottom-up' – from the data relating to individuals, according to how similar their value sets are.

In one sense, every archetype is a simple invention. Archetypes don't really exist 'out there,' they are statistical clusters of people with similar values, the size and shape of which are defined by the statistical rules used to create them. The rules define what 'similar'

By starting with the values of the individual and then overlaying specific brand or behavioral data on top, we can slice and dice this data in every imaginable way (as long as the original overlay data has been collected). By statistically comparing the values of one group with those of another it is possible to visualize the key differences between them, thereby providing a common foundation and a 'shared language' for all future work.

actually means. Just how 'similar' is a pragmatic decision. For example, it is mathematically possible to divide any population into just two mega-clusters, though each mega-cluster would bring together so many different people that it would have very few practical uses. On the other hand, it would be possible to create a new cluster for every exact pattern of answers to the questions in the statement battery. In this case, every individual would create a cluster of his or her own: the chances of two individuals answering every question in exactly the same way are vanishingly small. Generally speaking, then, we combine statistical modeling with common sense to identify between five and ten clusters that fit well together, mathematically speaking (that is, with a low error rate).

Figure 3.9 shows the eight main archetypes among German consumers. Below we describe the main characteristics of these archetypes in some detail to illustrate the level of understanding that can be reached via archetype analysis. Using this approach we can combine highly qualitative insights into peoples' attitudes, preferences, and lifestyles with hard demographic and economic data, all on the basis of robust data. To help communication, it is possible to use photographs of people who sum up their archetypes: a particular age, sex, style of clothing, and so on. It is this holistic view of different segments of the population that makes such cluster or archetype analysis so useful.

The following analysis is based on German data, but different countries have different archetypes, and different numbers of archetypes. In Greece, for example, seven archetypes stand out, rather than eight. Portugal has nine.

Archetypes are just one way of clustering and analyzing the data obtained from individuals' values profiles. Archetypes can be very useful in some circumstances, but they may not be appropriate in others. It all depends on the marketing problems and priorities of the brand and company in question.

When it comes to using archetypes, flexibility and pragmatic decision making are key. Any and every population can be divided into its own bespoke archetypes. Every country has its archetypes. For more detailed analysis, smaller populations – such as 'hotel users' or 'women between 18 and 35' – can be broken down into their particular archetypes.

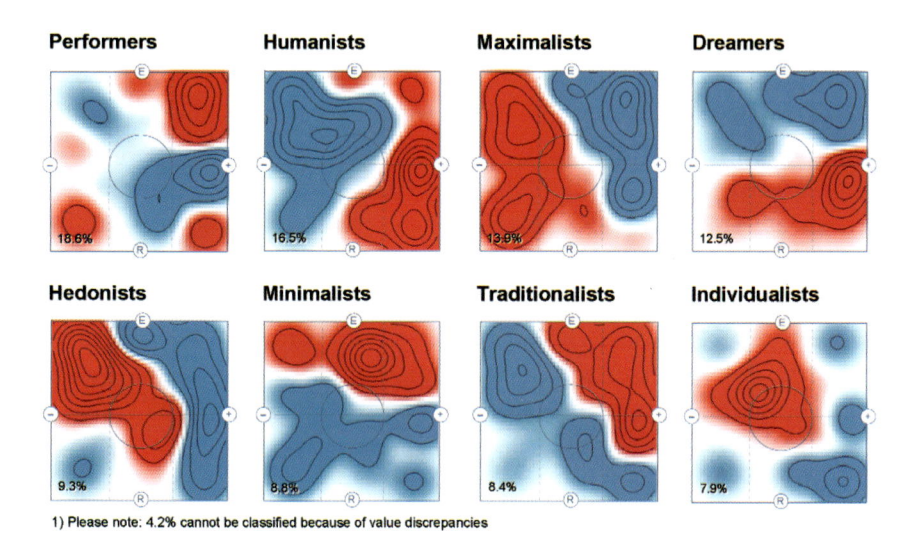

1) Please note: 4.2% cannot be classified because of value discrepancies

Figure 3.9 The eight main German consumer archetypes
Source: Roland Berger Strategy Consultants, Forsa data (Germany, April 2004, n=1500, population 14+, CATI)

Performers

Performers' values cluster mainly in the progressive and traditional performance parts of the grid – with a strong rejection of progressive

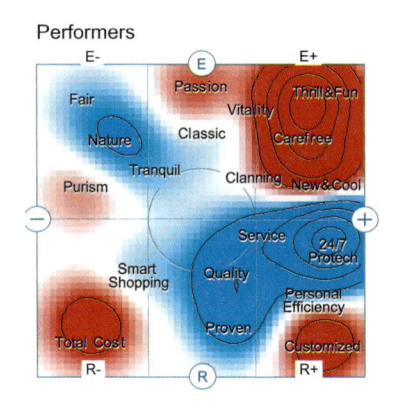

hedonist values. The strongest preference is for the value 24/7 protech; the strongest aversion is against Thrill and fun.

Performers represent 18.6 percent of the total population, making them the largest archetype in Germany. Their average age is 45, and they are slightly over-represented among males (53 percent are male). Of this archetype, 60 percent are married and 70 percent are employed, making them the largest group within the working population. They also tend to be relatively well paid: 56 percent earn more than €2500 a month, 22 percent more than €4000, and only 7 percent have an income below €1000.

Performers do not experiment or take risks. They do not try out new things, set trends or behave in an egocentric manner. On the contrary, Performers place a great deal of value on service and quality, and have a strong tendency to rely on tested solutions. Performers do not act spontaneously, but plan things in advance. They are disciplined, structured and well organized. Given their lack of cost or price awareness, Performers also have a very strong technological and somewhat pro-spending attitude. Performers are highly rational by nature and do not request tailor-made, efficient solutions or offers. As such, they do not seek attention.

Humanists

Humanists live mainly in the altruist, moneyist and traditional hedonist parts of the grid. They are most strongly averse to the progressive performance values clustering in the bottom right-hand part.

Humanists are the second largest archetype within the German

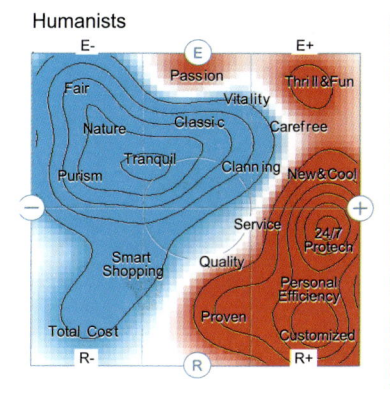

population: 16.5 percent. They are drawn particularly towards the values Tranquil and Nature while rejecting 24/7 pro-tech and Customized. With an average age of 50, they are likely to be women (63 percent of humanists are female, 37 percent male). Only about half are employed, and overall they have the lowest income (15 percent earn less than €1000 per month, and only 37 percent have an income above €2500, with only 10 percent above €4000).

Humanists have a strong sense of right and wrong, and live their lives by their moral values. They reject the materialism of modern society, and unlike Performers, have very little faith that new technologies will solve society's problems, focusing more on the downsides and dangers of technology than its benefits. Humanists don't like showiness. They positively reject image-led marketing, are not interested in fashion and are not ambitious careerists. Instead, they look inwards to their own thoughts, feelings and beliefs, preferring to spend time with people who share their attitudes. Because of their strong beliefs, they are likely to be active in the local community. As shoppers, they are highly price-conscious but they are also likely to choose ethical, green and 'authentic' products or services and to favor non-traditional retail formats.

Maximalists

Maximalists live mainly in the progressive hedonist part of the grid, with strong tinges of traditional hedonism and progressive performance. They are averse to altruist and moneyist values.

Maximalists are drawn particularly towards Thrill and fun and Personal efficiency, while rejecting Nature and Total cost. They

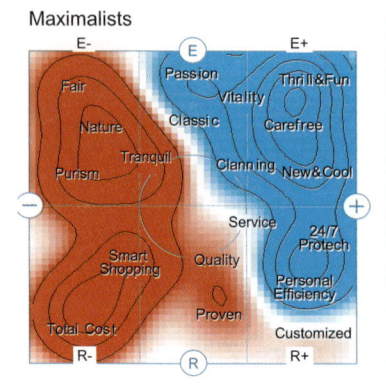

represent 13.9 percent of the population and are the second youngest archetype, with an average age of 35. They are slightly likelier to be male (males account for 56 percent of the group) and tend to be single. Of those that are married (only about one third are), many fall into the 'double income no kids' category. Most (56 percent) are employed, and apart from Performers, they are the most affluent archetype: 52 percent have an income exceeding €2500 per month and 20 percent exceeding €4000.

For Maximalists, life is about having one rich experience after another. Maximalists want to live life to the full, focusing on the fun of the moment rather than working to a 'life plan' or being guided by ethical or moral considerations. For them, image and show are important – they are avid buyers of premium brands and use them as a means of personal expression. They are dedicated followers of fashion. They are happy to spend large sums of money to attain the right lifestyle. They are keen to be 'in' with the in-crowd, and stay clear of traditional, social or environmental concerns that might cramp their style. The bright lights of the city are a strong magnet for them: the last thing they want to do is 'go back to nature.' Because they are so focused on the moment, Maximalists are also impatient. They hate queues, for example. And they love the 'new' of new technology, especially if it helps them save time as well as experience new things.

Dreamers

Dreamers live in the progressive hedonist, traditional hedonist and altruist regions of the grid. They are particularly averse to progressive performance values.

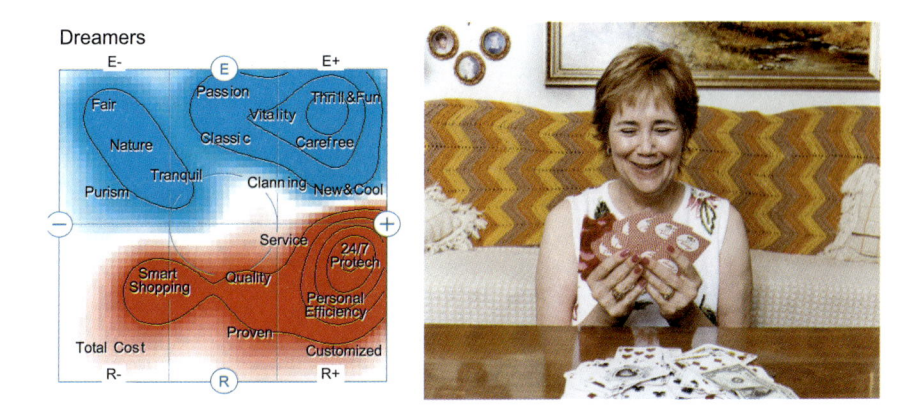

Dreamers represent 12.5 percent of the population. They are drawn particularly towards Thrill and fun and Nature, while rejecting 24/7 pro-tech and Smart shopping. On average, they are in their late 40s and tend to be female (57 percent). Almost 60 percent are married and around a half are employed. Of this archetype, 15 percent earn less than €1000 per month, and only 37 percent have an income exceeding €2500, with 10 percent earning above €4000.

Dreamers are a more relaxed, socially aware version of Maximalists. Their main concern in life is not to 'succeed' in the future but to enjoy themselves now. New technologies' promise of improved functionality and efficiency leaves them cold, whereas the warmth of community gives them deep satisfaction. Concern about others, including the natural world, is part of their make-up. Earning lots of money and fitting into social norms is not top of their personal agendas: they prefer calmness and tranquillity to the stress involved in 'getting on.' So on average, they are not well off. As rejecters of a scientific, rational outlook on life, they are not 'smart' shoppers either. For them, the experience of consumption is more important than getting a bargain, or making sure the product or service is the best option on the market.

Hedonists

Hedonists live mainly in the progressive hedonist and progressive performance parts of the grid, rejecting altruist values, and the most common values of Service and Quality in the grid's center.

Hedonists represent 9.3 percent of the population. They are particularly drawn towards Passion and 24/7 pro-tech, while particularly

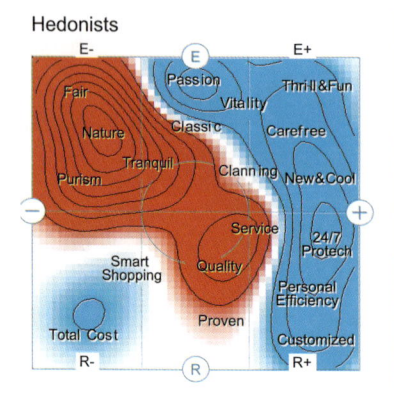 

rejecting Nature, Fair, and Purism. They are the youngest archetype, with an average age of 26 (so they are predominantly single, with only 22 percent married). They are 61 per cent male. Only 48 percent are employed. Although many are students, a significant proportion earn more than €4000 a month, making them the third-highest income group overall.

The hallmark of the Hedonist is that he (Hedonists are mainly male) rejects the most commonly accepted values such as service and quality. Indeed, for Hedonists 'breaking the rules' is one of the ways they express themselves: these people are most likely to be found among alternative and trendy sub-cultures. One downside to their personalities is their tendency to be narcissistic and attention seeking, but they make up for this with their passionate enthusiasm. For the Hedonist anything conventional or traditional is by definition bad, while anything new is by definition 'cool.' This extends to new technologies, especially those that provide access to 'any time, anywhere' information and experiences. As the same time, Hedonists are cost-conscious. Altruistic values such as 'nature,' 'fair,' and 'tranquil' arouse their positive hostility: they are self-centred and not socially concerned.

Minimalists

Minimalists are almost the exact opposite of Dreamers, living in the moneyist and performance (traditional and progressive) parts of the grid – all the values rejected by Dreamers. Minimalists in turn reject hedonist values.

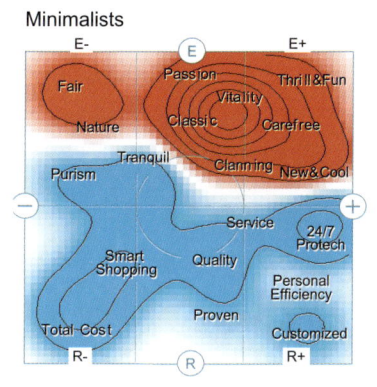

Minimalists represent 8.8 percent of the population. They are particularly attracted to Total cost and 24/7 pro-tech while rejecting Vitality and Fair. They average 42 years of age and around 60 percent are male. They are the second most likely archetype to be employed (60 percent), but only have an average income.

Minimalists are almost the polar opposite of Dreamers. The thrill-seeking, fun-loving, experience-rich life is not for them. What they want instead is peace and quiet, order and efficiency, and everything kept to its bare essentials: why waste time and money buying expensive food for lunch when a home-made sandwich is just as good? Minimalists extend this low-emotion, rational approach to all aspects of their lives. They take a low profile, avoiding the limelight and rejecting all signs of showiness. They like new technology because they believe it can help them organize their lives better. They opt for products that they believe to be reliable and that will last – and may well repair them if they break down, rather than replacing them with a new one. They are also ruthlessly smart shoppers: extremely price-conscious and scornful of razzmatazz, image-led marketing. Others might criticize their lives for being narrow and limited, but they don't care. They like their secure, orderly life.

Traditionalists

Traditionalists live in the altruist and traditional performance parts of the grid while particularly rejecting progressive hedonist values.

Traditionalists account for 8.4 percent of the population. They are particularly attracted to Nature, Quality, and Customized while rejecting

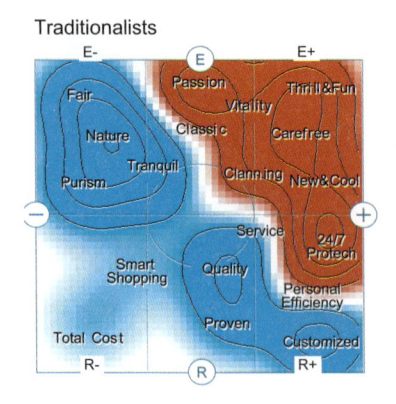 

24/7 pro-tech, Carefree, and Passion. They are the oldest archetype (average age 55), and tend to be female (59 percent). They are mostly married (70 percent) and 53 percent are employed. Very few Traditionalists are rich (only 37 percent earn more than €2500 a month, and only 10 percent more than €4000), though overall their income is average.

Traditionalists are the most conservative of the archetypes. They tend to be older, with an average – but not high – income, and look for traditional values in things and society: quality, reliability, authority, discipline, routine. They are skeptical of new technologies, believing they tend to make things more complex rather than simpler. They look for peace and quiet in their lives, strongly disapproving of carefree, fun-seeking attitudes and disliking all sorts of showiness. Instead, they seek the timeless continuity of community and nature.

Individualists

Individualists are attracted to all the extreme values at the edge of the grid while rejecting the traditional values in the middle.

Individualists account for 7.9 percent of the population. They are particularly attracted by the value of Customization while rejecting all the values clustered around Tranquil. They have an average age of 36 years, and tend to be men (54 percent are male). Most are not married (60 percent) and 55 percent are employed. Individualists' income varies widely (14 percent earn less than €1000 a month, but on the other hand, 41 percent earn more than €2500 and 12 percent more than €4000).

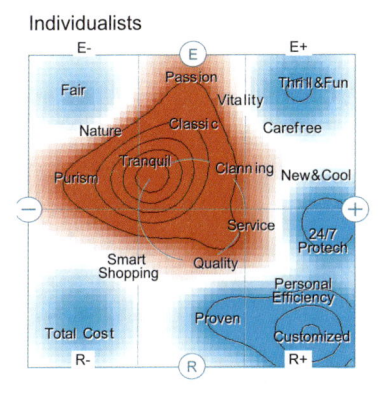
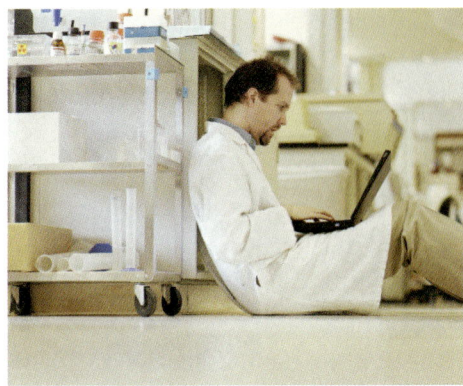

The one thing Individualists can't stand is 'peace and quiet.' For them, a stress-free life is a boring life. But while a part of them is attracted to high-adrenalin, adventurous activities, what really interests them is personal achievement – not because they crave the admiration of others, but because they want to make the most of their own talents. So they seek out technologies and situations that fit their own priorities and interests, and are always scanning the horizon for interesting new challenges. This strong focus on personal achievement – along with an obvious lack of interest in conventional social norms – means Individualists are not great socializers. Also, they are not interested in brands as means of self-expression or 'badging', though excellent performance, scientific proof and superior functionality are always pluses for them. In keeping with this rationalistic approach to life, they have a tendency to be price-conscious.

We'll see later how entire brand strategies can be developed around a decision to target some archetypes and not others. The tricks are to identify which archetypes the brand is best at attracting, and to understand the potential economic value of each archetype. This analysis can be done relatively easily because factors such as income and willingness to spend money are 'attached' to the original values data when the research is first conducted.

Please note: any brand that decides to appeal to a particular value is likely to appeal to more than one archetype. Figure 3.10 shows four of the German archetypes discussed above. Any brand targeting the value Customized would attract them all (as shown by the boxes). A brand targeting the values Customized *and* 24/7 pro-tech (boxes and circles) would successfully attract the Hedonists, Minimalists, and Individualists – but would now risk putting off the Traditionalists, who have a positive aversion to 24/7 pro-tech. A brand targeting Customized and 24/7 pro-tech and also making a point of being anti-Fair would be even more attractive to both the Hedonists and Minimalists (triangles). But the chances of alienating the Traditionalists would now be much greater because they are deeply committed to Fair values. Later on, we will see how identifying a small number of core values can create a values backbone: a brand can then clearly target two or three different archetypes. This underlines the need for crystal-clear brand strategies, and a deep understanding of the values – and people – the brand is trying to address.

Archetype analysis can reveal important differences across countries and regions. Working with the same error rates (that is, the same propensity to 'cluster'), we find different numbers and types of archetypes in different countries, as well as different proportions of the population belonging to each archetype. While basic 'building block' values may be similar across Europe, for example, the combinations of values held by different groups of people tend to differ in, say, the German market or the Greek market. The Portuguese market naturally breaks down into nine, rather than eight archetypes (see Figure 3.11).

However, sometimes general population archetypes such as those described above have little relevance. Some markets may need to create their own bespoke archetypes, built around their particular customer bases. For example, the eight general archetypes listed

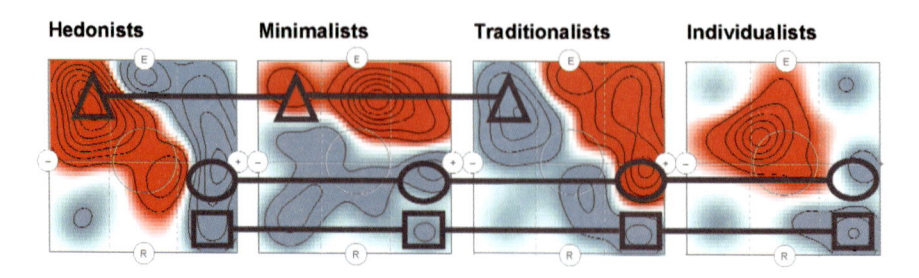

Figure 3.10 How values overlap across different archetypes
Source: Roland Berger Strategy Consultants, Forsa data (Germany, April 2004, n=1500, population 14+, CATI)

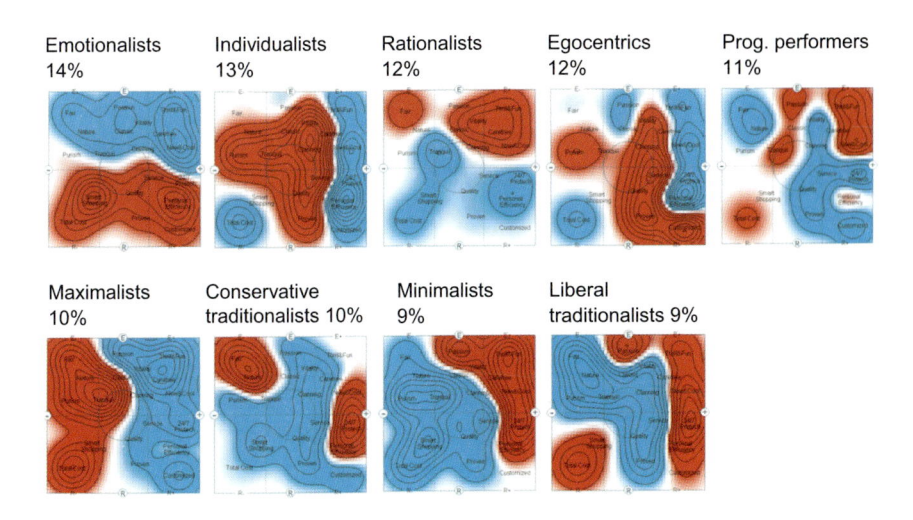

| Emotionalists 14% | Individualists 13% | Rationalists 12% | Egocentrics 12% | Prog. performers 11% |

| Maximalists 10% | Conservative traditionalists 10% | Minimalists 9% | Liberal traditionalists 9% |

Figure 3.11 The nine main Portuguese consumer archetypes
Source: Roland Berger Strategy Consultants, Metris data (Portugal, June 2004, n=2650, population 12–65 years, CATI)

above might not be relevant to a maker of breast implants for breast cancer patients, but there might be three or four different groups of patients with very different values affecting their approach to this highly specialized market.

SUMMARY

In Chapters 1 and 2 we discussed the many operational and strategic mistakes companies make when attempting to manage their brands. In this chapter we have started to outline an alternative approach to brand management that starts with the customers' values rather than with companies' products or goals. We have shown how values profiles can be constructed, using hard data, to understand the values of individuals and segments.

Starting the brand-building process with the values of individuals and target groups delivers some important practical advantages. To remind you, this approach is:

◆ Not brand-centric. It looks at people first, and then asks how well a brand does, or doesn't, fit into their lives. It puts the brand in a broader and much more realistic perspective, which most brand-driven market research does not.

◆ Hugely flexible. Because each individual has a mathematically calculated 'values signature,' this data can be used as an 'atomic' building block in almost any conceivable analysis: connecting values to age, income, social class, or region for example. Or connecting values to category usage, brand preference, media consumption habits, shopping habits, brand preferences, and so on.

◆ Fact-based. Discussion of people's values (and connected attitudes and behaviors) is based on hard, statistically significant data.

Having investigated the underlying methodology, we have identified two more benefits. Values profiles:

◆ Turn hard-to-grasp difficult-to-explain information about highly qualitative issues into a visual aid that everyone can 'see.' It's difficult, if not impossible, for human brains to deal with 19 different data points at one time. But it's very easy to 'see' this information if it is laid out in the right way.

◆ Aid communication between departments within the company and with agencies. The analysis, and its visual representation, help to create a common understanding and a common language for all of those involved in strategy development and execution. Everyone can look at the same picture and say, 'Do you see how this is different from that?'

But so far we have only taken the first step. We have seen how people's values – a highly emotional and subjective thing – can be turned into hard, objective, comparative data. The next step is to apply this methodology to understand brands and markets. We turn to this challenge in Chapter 5, but before we do so we need to answer another question. Does values profiling work in B2B markets too?

4 Profiling values in a B2B context

Values-based brand management

In Chapter 3 we introduced the logic and methodology of values profiling, and most of the examples we gave came from consumer markets. It may not seem obvious but the same basic approach applies equally well to business-to-business (B2B) marketing. The number and type of values demonstrated may be different, but a values-based approach still works.

There are some differences in methodology: instead of identifying the values of individuals, this approach generates a profile of the values of people working within a particular business. Archetype analysis differs too: every business market generates its own archetypes. Nevertheless (as case studies in later chapters demonstrate) it is our experience that

Table 4.1 The 15 business values at the heart of all business decisions

Loyalty	Ownership cost
Integrity	Purchase price
Empathy	Durability
Experience	Service competence
Solidity	Innovation
Commitment	Customization
Simplicity	Precision
Excellence	

analyzing businesses by their values yields as many insights and recipes for useful action as it does in consumer markets.

Figure 4.1 shows the values grid of a typical B2B market. Both the grid and the values are different, but the basic approach is the same.

The grid

Instead of moving along a spectrum from less to more consumption and from rational to emotional, the axes of the B2B grid are degrees of complexity, and tangible versus intangible value. This creates four key quadrants of:

◆ Security

◆ Trust

◆ Cost

◆ Performance.

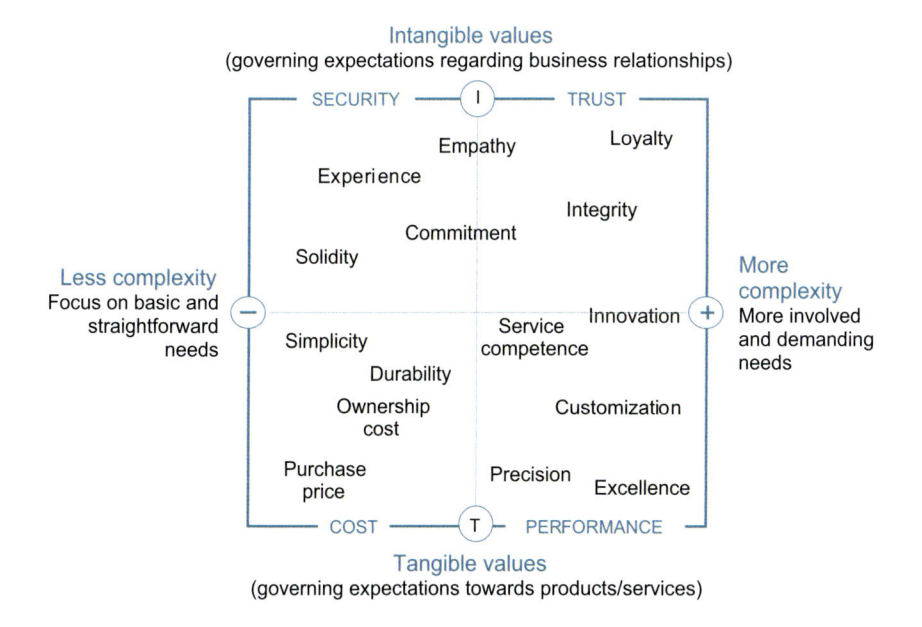

Intangible values
(governing expectations regarding business relationships)

Figure 4.1 The main B2B values and grid
Source: Roland Berger Strategy Consultants

The values

While many of the values are similar, they are not exactly the same. When companies' values are researched, business people end up espousing 15 (as opposed to consumers' core 19) different values. They include Loyalty and Integrity in the trust quadrant, and Experience and Solidity in the security quadrant, with Empathy and Commitment on the borderline between the two. The performance quadrant includes Innovation, Service competence, Customization, Precision, and Excellent, while the cost quadrant includes Simplicity, Ownership cost, Purchase price, and Durability.

Once individual companies' value profiles have been identified we can apply the same analytical approach, placing the values on a grid (see Figure 4.1), and visualizing the company's values by the degree to which it conforms to or is distant from the average. Like the consumer profile, this creates quadrants which bring certain values together.

Figure 4.2 shows the profile of one individual company. It shows that:

◆ The company is extremely cost conscious. To always obtain the lowest possible price is the key decision criterion even if that means sacrificing product quality or features.

◆ The company is systematically risk averse in its business relationships – it requires sound and stable business partners with good references.

◆ The company is less than averagely focused on obtaining above-average performance in the products and services it purchases. Reliable and consistent execution, long-lastingness, and any kind of customer service are sacrificed to achieve a lower price.

◆ The company places little if any value on trust-conveying dimensions such as Integrity and Loyalty. That means that long-term business relationships with partners willing to go the extra mile in terms of service are not valued. Instead, the company is looking

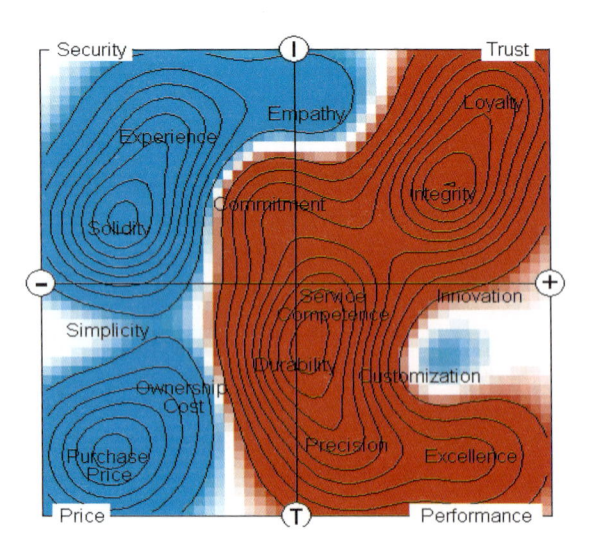

Figure 4.2 Value profile of an individual company
Source: Roland Berger Strategy Consultants, Metris data (Portugal, October 2004, n=778, business market)

for short-term price and cost optimization, not fair and equal win–win business partnerships.

As with consumers, different brands, markets and industries can be compared. Figure 4.3 shows the value profiles of Portuguese companies segmented by size and by industry. It is remarkable how different the values of small and home office (SOHO) businesses are from small and medium-sized enterprises. Similarly the value patterns of construction, hotel and restaurant, and wholesale companies vary greatly.

Archetype analysis can also be used to analyze B2B markets. For example, Figure 4.4 identifies the five main values archetypes found among Portuguese telecoms businesses. (There is an important point to note here. Among consumers, archetypes are common across

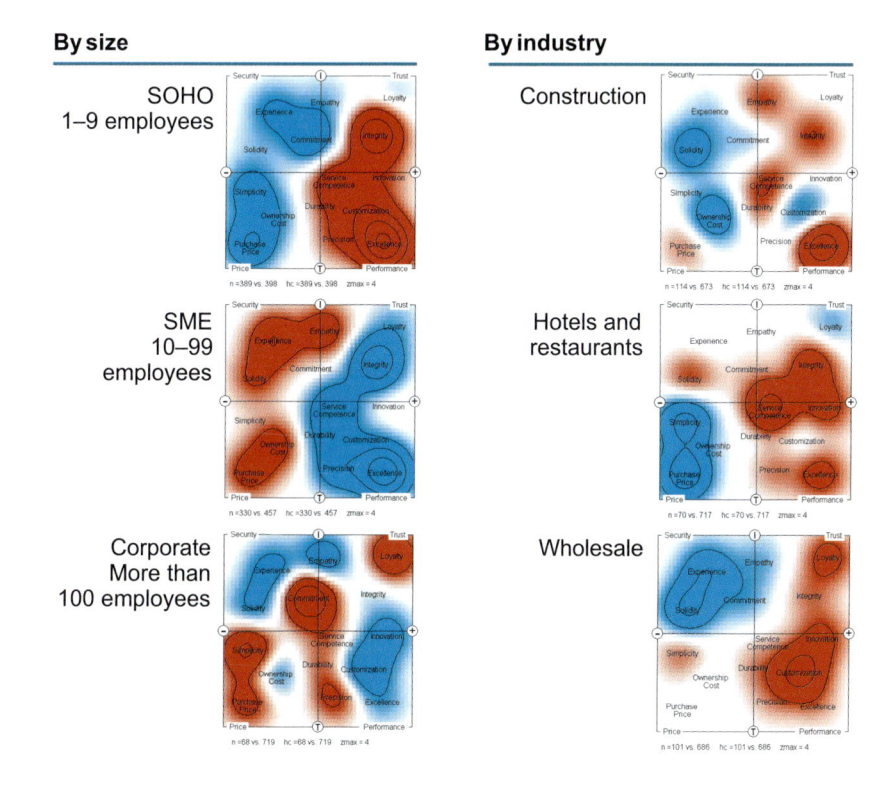

Figure 4.3 The value profiles of companies by size and sector (Portugal)
Source: Roland Berger Strategy Consultants, Metris data (Portugal, October 2004, n=778, business market)

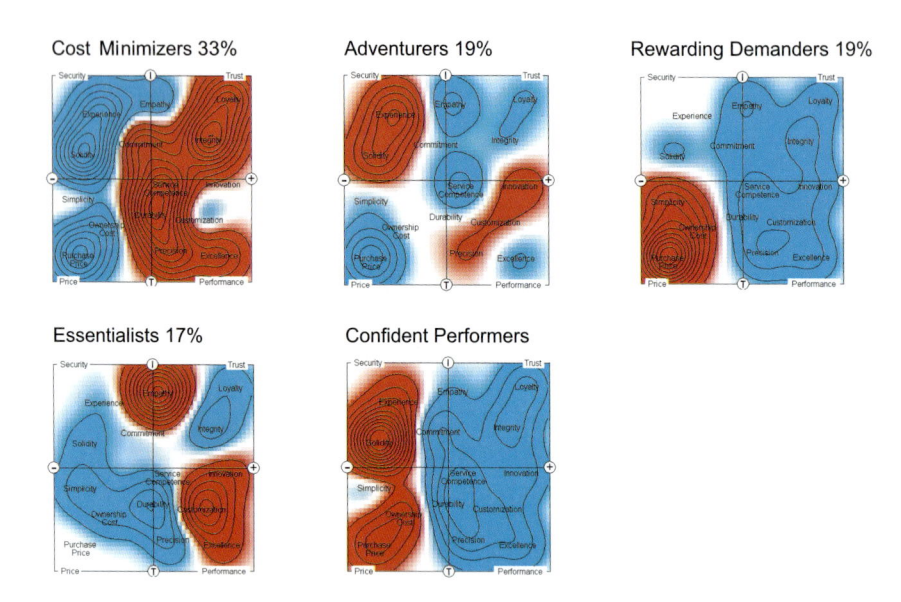

Figure 4.4 The five main Portuguese archetypes in the telecoms market
Source: Roland Berger Strategy Consultants, Metris data (Portugal, October 2004, n=778, business market)

categories – it is the same consumer whether he or she is buying cars, or soaps, or pensions. But every industry throws up its own archetypes. The archetypes emerging from the Portuguese telecoms market will therefore be different from those in the German engineering or UK financial services market.)

By far the biggest group (33 percent) are the Cost Minimizers, who are strongly attracted towards Total cost and Solidity, while rejecting Durability and Integrity. Adventurers (19 percent) are attracted to Total cost, Empathy, and Service competence, while rejecting Experience and Solidity. Rewarding Demanders (19 percent) are generally attracted to all the values in the Trust and Performance quadrants while positively rejecting Cost considerations. Essentialists (17 percent) focus on all the values of Ownership cost, Simplicity, and Durability, while rejecting those associated with Precision, Excellence, and Empathy. Like Rewarding Demanders, Confident Performers (12 percent) are attracted to all the values in the Trust and Performance quadrants, but unlike Rewarding Demanders they reject the values of Experience and Solidity.

SUMMARY

It is traditional to see consumer markets as tending to be more 'emotional' and therefore more obviously influenced by values, while B2B markets are seen as tending to be more rational and therefore (arguably) less influenced by values. Nevertheless different businesses do have different values, and these values have a marked effect on their attitudes and behaviors. Businesses that value innovation prioritize different things from those that value integrity, and these in turn have different priorities from those that value excellence. Understanding the values of the business we are serving is crucial to developing a value proposition that the customer really wants. That is the next challenge: having identified and understood our customers' values, how can we turn this insight into actions that will deliver positive results?

5 Turning values information into insight

Values-based brand management

Back in Chapter 2 we discussed the need for a new Ariadne-thread for marketing: something that unifies and integrates different sources of data, different people with their different specialist skills, and different processes (such as new product development or advertising), all into one consistent, seamless whole. We identified a candidate – understanding customer values – and, holding it tight, we took our first tentative steps into the marketing maze. We discovered how it is possible to turn 'soft' issues such as values into hard, comparable, easy-to-visualize information about people and groups.

This same values-based data can also be used to generate new insights into brands and markets. We can use it to understand:

- What drives markets. What are the values of the people who participate in this market (as opposed to those who choose not to)?

- Who buys brands. What are the values of the people who buy our brand and those of our rivals?

- Brand 'fit.' How does the brand's profile align, or not align, with the market's drivers?

- Brand differentiators. How do the values of the people who buy our brand differ from the rest of those participating in the market?

MARKET DRIVERS

Let's start with markets. Is there anything new to say about markets? Haven't they already been researched to death, by their size, their value, their growth, their technical attributes, and so on? Marketers already know whether their brand's buyers are young or old, male or female, rich or poor. So what's new? The answer of course is values: the values of the people who choose to participate in the market compared with those who choose not to. *What are the values that 'drive' the market?*

Starting at the wrong place

Most brand management processes start with either the product (or service) or a target market which has previously been identified as economically attractive. The natural next step is to address the question: 'How can we attract and win over this target market to maximize sales?'

The problem with this approach is that it *jumps to conclusions*. The methodology outlined in this chapter answers the core question better – but only because it starts with *facts*: facts about the users of the brand; facts which are independent of what the company's brand managers want or intend to do.

Figure 5.1 illustrates the values of buyers in three very different markets. Remember, all such values profiles tease out statistically significant differences between one group and another. For the purposes of this 'market driver' analysis, the difference in question is between those who participate in the market by buying the product, and those who do not.

Compared with non-buyers, for example, British mobile phone users reject 'altruistic' values such as Fair and Nature and are not driven by price. They are, however, particularly attracted to values such as Carefree, 24/7 pro-tech, plus closely associated values such as Thrill and fun and Personal efficiency. One immediate implication is that any brand opting to take a strongly pro-environmental or price-oriented stand is unlikely to appeal to existing market participants (though, of course, there is always the possibility that it might attract new entrants to the market).

If we compare these values with those of German beer drinkers we see instantly how different the market drivers/value profiles are. But subtle differences are important too. The values profiles of British mobile phone users and Japanese luxury cosmetic users seem very similar, for example, but note how Japanese cosmetic users are attracted towards the value Proven. Any company wanting to build a brand in this market would clearly be missing a trick if it failed to address this core user concern.

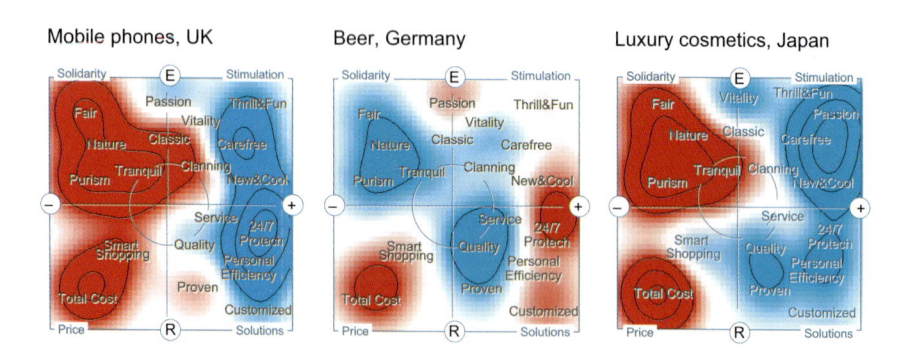

Figure 5.1 The values of market participants compared
Source: Roland Berger Strategy Consultants, data from Ipsos, Metris, Emnid (UK, PT, D, Aug/Oct/Nov 2001, n*=1.500, population 15–65 years, CATI)

By the way, Figure 5.1 illustrates another point about values profiling. It uses a crude four-segment quadrant to identify broad themes of price orientation, a yearning for social solidarity, for stimulation, or solutions, rather than tighter themes such as progressive hedonism or traditional performance which were introduced in Chapter 3. Depending on current priorities and market circumstances, alternative grids and frameworks of analysis can be deployed.

Figure 5.1 does beg one question, however: how do we know we have chosen the right definition of 'the market'? For example, some markets such as groceries and banking are so huge that they encompass the entire population. Clearly, analyzing the values of the entire population is not going to generate huge amounts of insight into the dynamics of these particular markets.[1] One of the advantages of this tool is its flexibility: the data can be sliced and diced – 'played with' – until interesting or significant patterns and differences emerge. Drilling down to the next level of detail can be extremely helpful.

Take the hotel market (Figure 5.2). The values of people using hotels for business purposes and the values of people using hotels for leisure purposes differ strikingly. A quick look at the two figures shows why it is difficult for the same hotel to serve both markets. Business users want a high standard of service, and rational criteria dominate when they choose between hotels. Further research into specifics will reveal that business customers greatly value efficiency, so fast check-in and check-out procedures and good technical facilities in rooms will be appreciated. Emotional values are a much greater influence among leisure users. These emotional preferences manifest themselves via a different list of priorities, including the general atmosphere of the hotel, style of room furnishings, and availability of facilities such as gyms and swimming pools.

---

1 Another case where market driver analysis offers limited extra insight is where the market is dominated by one particularly strong brand. In this case, the profile of category users is so similar to that of brand users that a different perspective is needed.

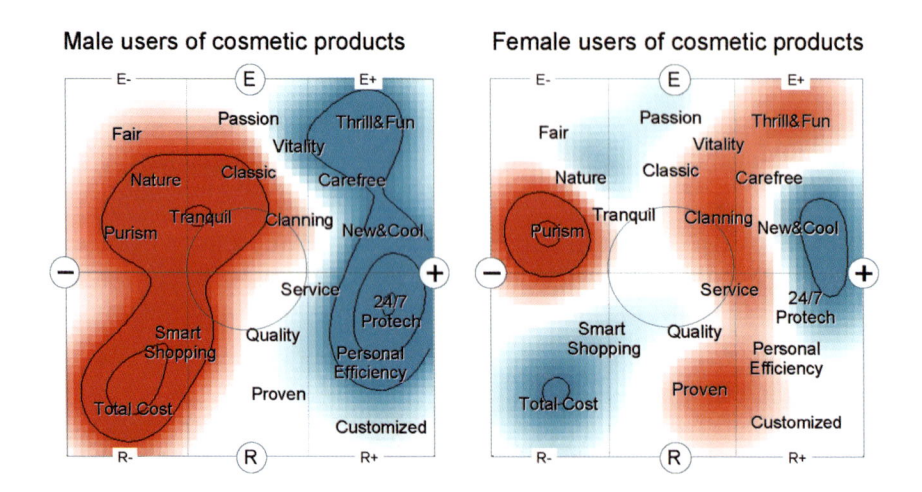

Figure 5.2 Contrasting values of German hotel users: business versus leisure
Source: Roland Berger Strategy Consultants, TNS Emnid data (Germany, September 2003, n=1500, population 14–65 years, CATI)

Figure 5.3 Values profiles of male and female users of personal hygiene and cosmetic products
Source: Roland Berger Strategy Consultants, Roland Berger Market Research data (Germany, March 2005, n=2004, population 16–69 years, CATI)

Figure 5.3 illustrates the value of 'drilling down into detail' in another way. Most consumers in European markets buy some sort of personal hygiene product, so at the level of the market as a whole the values profile tends to reflect that of the population as a whole. It doesn't generate many market-specific insights. However, simply by drilling down to the next level of detail – specifically, to the difference between males and females of a similar age group – we can highlight significant differences in underlying emotional drivers.

Total cost is an attraction while Thrill and fun is a turn-off. Men major much more strongly on values such as 24/7 pro-tech and Thrill and fun, while rejecting the altruist and moneyist values of Nature, Tranquil, Smart shopping, and Total cost. Such differences immediately suggest the types of product attributes and communications that are most likely to appeal. Misunderstand the values of those active in the market, and you are likely to misunderstand the market.

Figure 5.4 illustrates the same theme, this time applied to differences between users of electric and manual toothbrushes. The contrast could hardly be greater. The values espoused by electrical toothbrush users are not only much stronger (as shown by the higher number of contour lines), they're also almost a mirror image of manual toothbrush users.

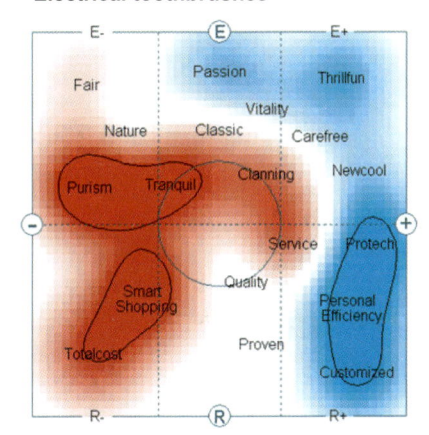

Figure 5.4 Values profile of users of different types of toothbrushes
Source: Roland Berger Strategy Consultants, TNS data (Hungary, September 2004, n=2011, population 14–70 years, CATI)

BRAND PROFILES

What really fascinates brand managers, however, is their own particular brand: what are the values of the users of my particular brand? Figure 5.5 illustrates the value profiles of customers using two powerful German grocery retailers, Aldi and Edeka. Aldi is a world-famous hard discounter, and compared with the rest of the German population (the comparison sample in this case), its customers are strongly oriented towards moneyist values, with a negative response to performance-oriented values such as Personal efficiency and even Service. Edeka, on the other hand, is the leading 'traditional' grocery store, and the profile of its customers shows a much greater orientation to traditional values: Service, Quality, Tranquil, and Classic. Compared with the average German shopper, Edeka customers are not price sensitive.

Remember, this brand profile – let's call it the brand's *actual value proposition* – is a simple statement of fact: these are the values of the people who buy this particular brand. Whether or not the brand is actually trying to target these particular people is a different matter, to which we will return later.

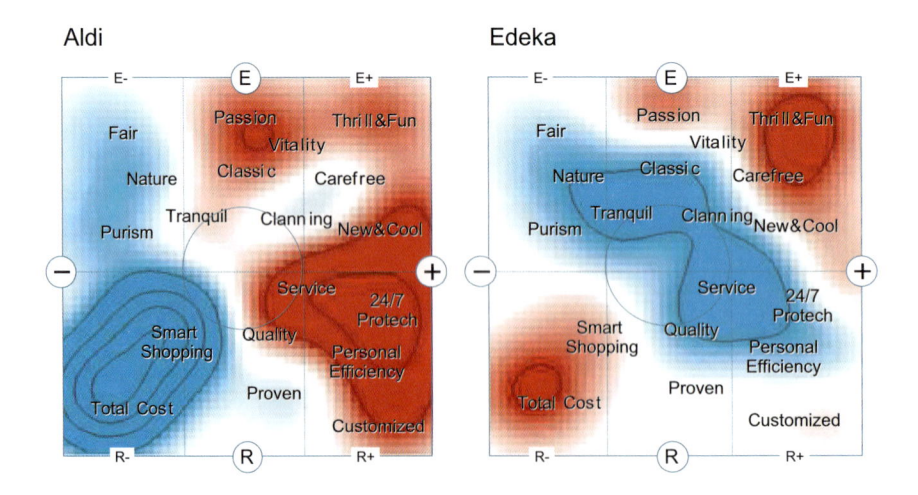

Figure 5.5 Two major brand profiles compared
Source: Roland Berger Strategy Consultants, Roland Berger Market Research data (Germany, March 2005, n=2004, population 16–69 years, CATI)

Reminder

A profile of a brand is a profile of the values of the users of that brand. It is not the 'values' brand managers wish to associate their brand with. Brand profiles are discovered by asking people first of all about their values, and then asking them which brands they use.

Not all brand profiles end up being so strong or different, however. Figure 5.6 compares the brand profiles of three famous car brands.

The basic profile of BMW buyers (in Germany) is quite similar to those of Audi, but the BMW brand emerges as much clearer. The profile of Opel is quite different from those of both BMW and Audi. Opel buyers are much more cost and price-conscious, and have a slight bias against 24/7 pro-tech attitudes. Also, Opel buyers' contour lines are not nearly as high as BMW buyers': the values of Opel buyers are not that different from the population as a whole. Generally speaking, brands with an extremely strong and clear profile are the most strongly differentiated.

There are many possible further permutations and combinations of such analysis. One obvious consideration is the degree to which a

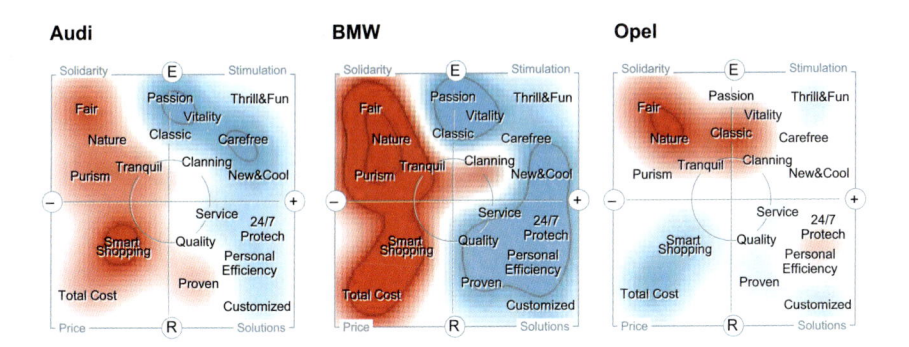

Figure 5.6 Brand profiles of different car brands in Germany
Source: Roland Berger Strategy Consultants, Roland Berger Market Research data (Germany, March 2005, n=2004, population 16–69 years, CATI)

73

brand's value profile differs from that of the market in which it competes. Here, the comparison is not with the population as a whole, but other market participants, thereby helping to highlight what differentiates the brand within that particular market.

Figure 5.7 gives an example from the German broadcasting market. The values of viewers of private television stations such as RTL and Pro7 are very different from those of viewers of the traditional public sector broadcasters ARD and ZDF.

Another way of comparing brands is to map their different brand profiles against the archetypes we introduced in the last chapter. Figure 5.8 shows one way of doing this, using what we call 'joint space mapping.' The map places different archetypes on the same grid, putting those archetypes that share a lot of values close together and those emphasizing different or opposing values further apart. Thus Dreamers and Humanists (using the German archetypes introduced in Chapter 2) have many shared values, but both have little in common with Individualists. If a brand's user profile

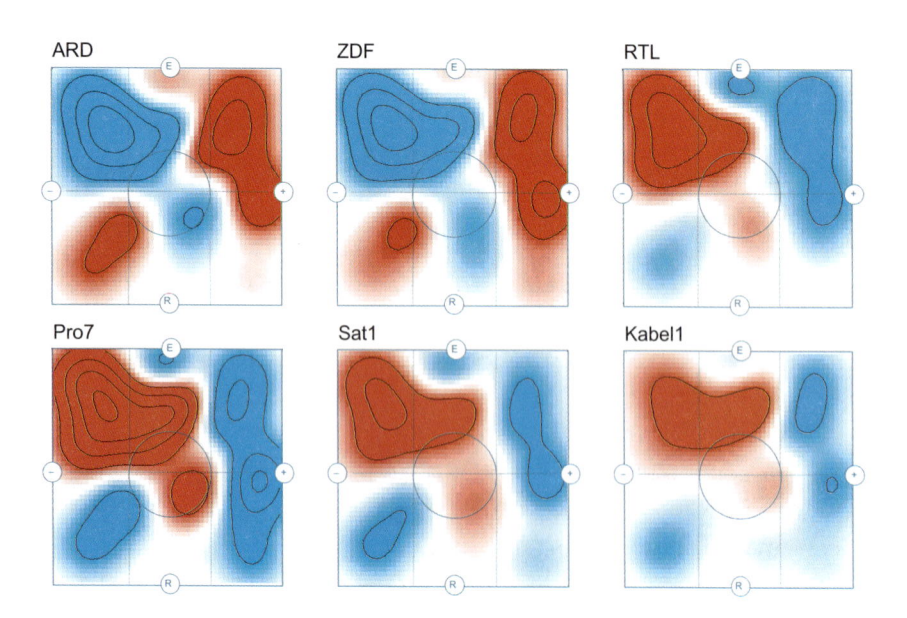

Figure 5.7 Brand differentiation, on the basis of brand buyers' values
Source: Roland Berger Strategy Consultants, Forsa data
(Germany, April 2004, n=1500, population 14+, CATI)

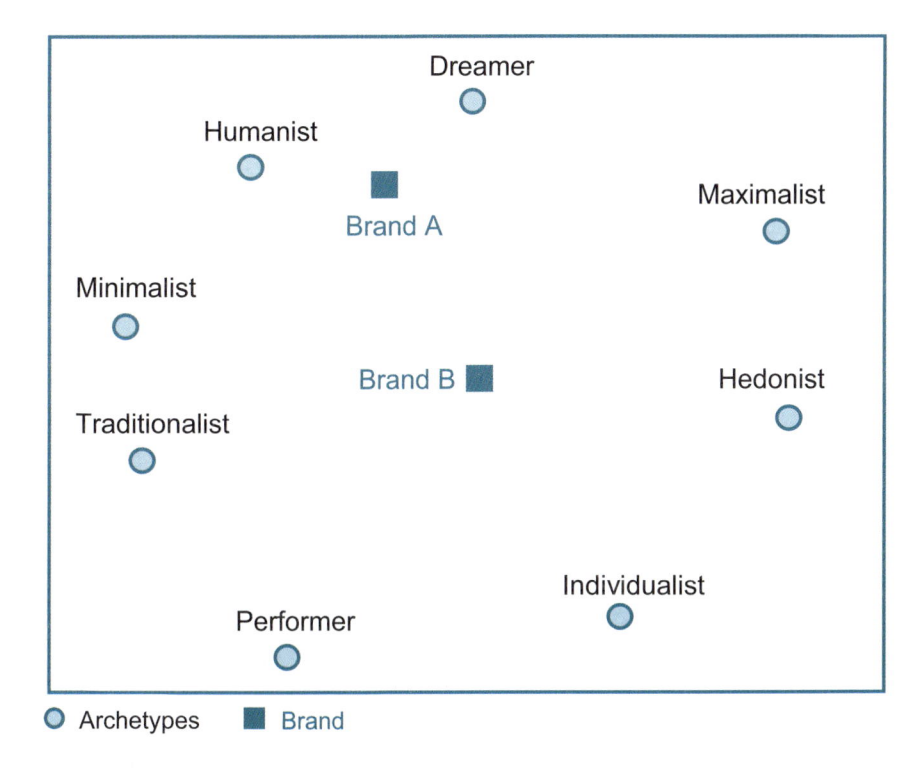

Figure 5.8 A simplified 'joint space map'
Source: Roland Berger Strategy Consultants

matched that of one archetype exactly, it would sit exactly on top of that archetype on the joint space map. If its user profile showed no bias towards any values archetype it would be placed exactly in the middle of the map. Thus, in this example, the users of Brand A particularly favor the values of Dreamers and Humanists, while the users of Brand B perfectly represent the population as a whole, rather than any particular segment.

In joint space maps, brands that serve everybody – such as grocers, banks, and gas stations – tend to cluster in the middle of the map, with very little to differentiate them. But in other markets, the power of certain archetypes becomes very clear.

Take the female personal hygiene and cosmetic market. It is strongly driven by emotional values such as Fair, Nature, Carefree, and Clanning, so most of the brands cluster in the 'northern' area of the map where the highly emotional values lie (Figure 5.9).

Feminine personal hygiene and cosmetic brands – Germany

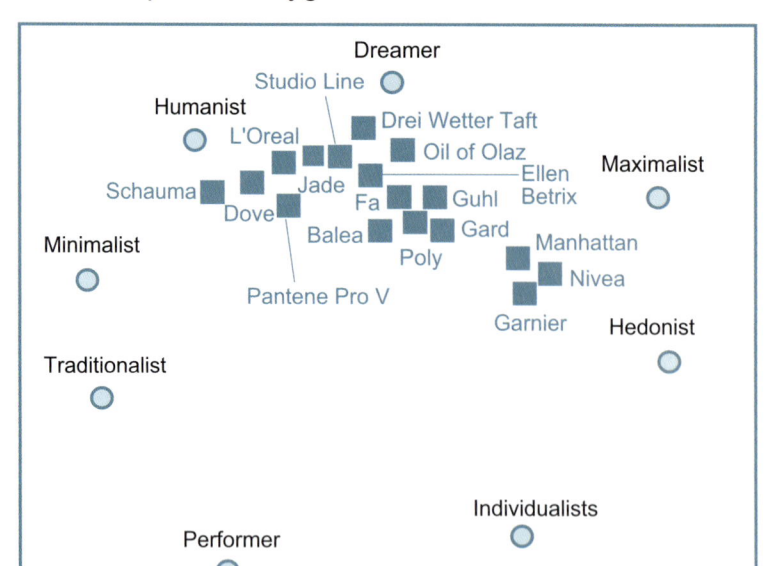

Figure 5.9 Mapping the competitive playing field for brands and archetypes
Source: Roland Berger Strategy Consultants, Roland Berger Market Research data
(Germany, March 2005, n=2004, population 16–69 years, CATI)

Within the overall market, however, different brands appeal more to some values than others. Some, such as L'Oreal and Schauma, attract buyers in the 'altruist' north-west quadrant of the map, while others, such as Garnier and Nivea, attract the hedonists in the north-east quadrant.

Visualizing the differences between brands' positions within complete markets in this way is a very simple and effective way of identifying opportunities and threats. (As ever, of course, such maps show the reality of which values archetypes brands actually appeal to, regardless of whether this appeal is deliberate or not.) Is there an opportunity for a female hygiene brand to completely shake off market tradition and appeal to the performer archetype? Or would it be better to tweak offerings or communications to attract more of one archetype, even if that risks losing the affection of another? We'll develop a way of quantifying answers to such questions in Chapter 6. But already the intuitive power of this tool is obvious.

Another angle of analysis is to start with particular groups of customers and to see how well, or badly, a brand's value profile 'fits' the values of the customers in question. Figure 5.10 shows the values profile of German consumers over the age of 60. It is a pretty distinctive profile: quite conservative (strong on values like Quality, Service, and Classic), and also favoring 'solidarity' values such as Fair and Nature. It then compares these values with the profiles of 12 major German brands.

Brands like Allianz and Deutsche Telekom show a good fit: they 'naturally' attract the over-60s. But brands such as Lufthansa, Ikea, and Vodafone are almost exact opposites. Such considerations are becoming especially important in Western European markets where

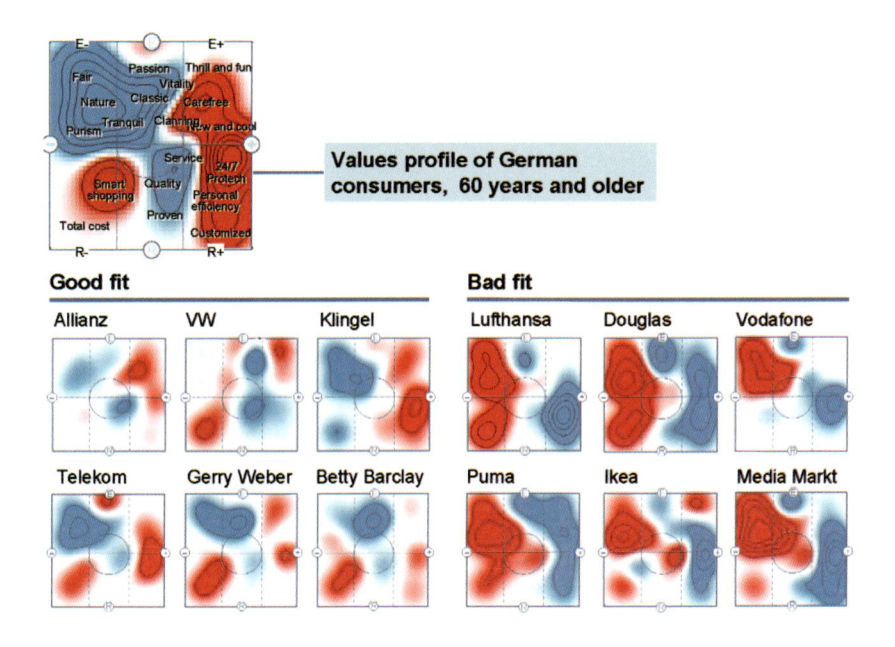

Figure 5.10 Are brands ignoring the over-60s?
Source: Roland Berger Strategy Consultants, Roland Berger Market Research data (Germany, March 2005, n=2004, population 16–69 years, CATI)

the ageing baby boomer generation represents a huge demographic change. In Germany for example, 32 percent of brands studied show a good fit with the values of 16–29-year-olds, with just 7 percent showing a good fit with the values of over-60s.[2] As we commented earlier, considering the spending power of the over-60s, this suggests that many brands are missing a major marketing opportunity.

Further analyses can throw light on a brand's evolution over time, and how it is perceived in different geographical markets. For example, Figure 5.11 shows how the values of the Portuguese mobile phone operator Telecel changed over a period of four years. When it was acquired, Telecel users were big on Tranquil, anti-Carefree, and New and cool – strange values for a mobile phone operator. Four years later, under the more 'emotional' Vodafone brand, the anti-Carefree and New and cool sentiments had been replaced by a clearly positive attachment to these values. The previous attraction to Tranquil and Total cost had also disappeared.

When it comes to managing a global or international brand, brand managers also need to understand its profile territory by territory.

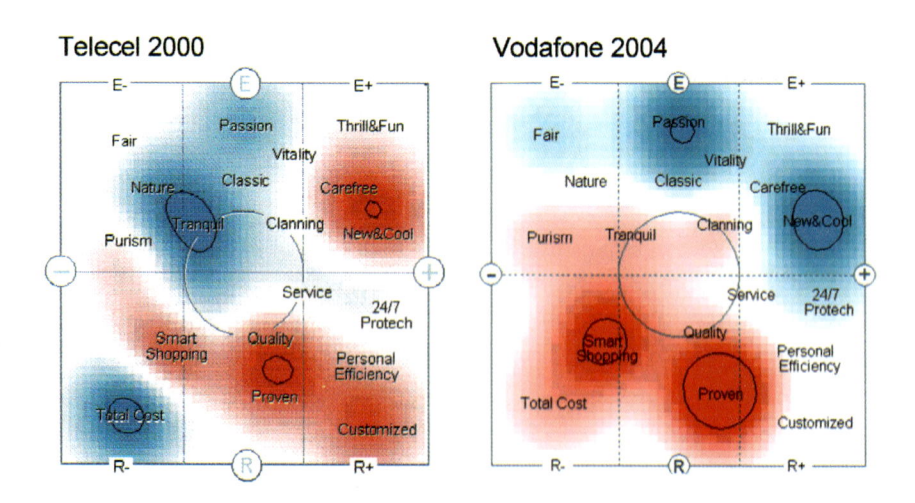

Figure 5.11 How Telecel's brand profile changed after it was acquired
Source: Roland Berger Strategy Consultants

---

2 Roland Berger *Brand Power* report, 2005.

Figure 5.12 shows how the profile of the Nike brand differs in the United Kingdom, Germany, and China. If a brand's profile differs greatly from market to market, then clearly, building a common global branding positioning with common marketing campaigns will be difficult. In this case, the brand profiles are pretty similar, but there are enough differences for brand managers to want to investigate further. In the United Kingdom, for instance, Thrill and fun hardly figures. In Germany, Quality is a turn-off. And the contour lines of the brand in China are much higher than in Germany and the United Kingdom where, perhaps, the Nike brand is not so strongly differentiated.

VALUES AND TRADITIONAL MARKET RESEARCH

The above examples show how analyzing brands and markets from a values perspective can open up a whole new world of possible insights. This is not 'instead of' traditional market research, but *as well as* it. The whole point of values profiling is to find *better* ways to use existing data; to better understand brands and markets. The 'trick,' if there is one, is to use the extra 'layer' of values information and analysis to create a unifying Ariadne-thread between three crucial levels of brand performance:

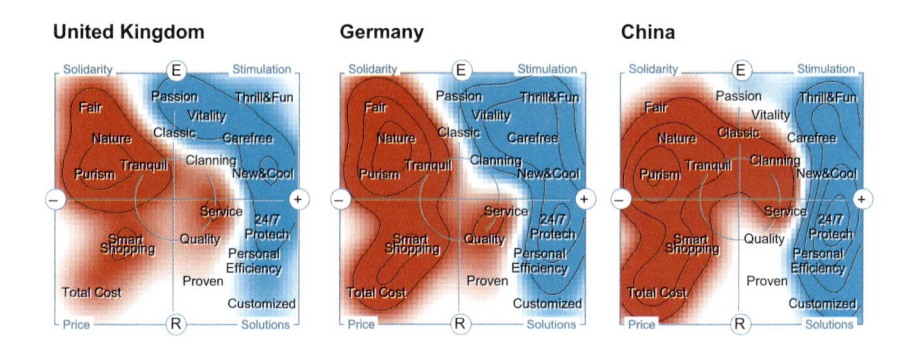

Figure 5.12 Nike's brand profile in three countries
Source: Roland Berger Strategy Consultants, data from Ipsos, Emnid, Gallup (UK, Germany, China, Aug/Oct/Nov 2001, n*=1500, population 15–65 years, CATI)

◆ its emotional appeal: how well it connects with the target market's values

◆ its functional appeal: how well its various functional attributes meet user requirements, *remembering that many of these practical and functional requirements are created, defined, and shaped by underlying values*

◆ quantitative and economic: assessing how changes in the first two levels will affect key metrics such as market share, margin, value growth, and lifetime customer value.

We discuss the emotional and functional levels in more detail in Chapter 6, when we look at strategy formulation. But right now, we want to stress the vital links between traditional market research and values research. They need to be integrated to create a seamless whole, and this integration needs to be 'built in' from the earliest stages of the original design of the research.

This creates a problem. We can only slice and dice data in the ways just discussed if the various data fields – brand values, brand usage, customer age, and so on – are linked together at the level of the individual. If this link is not present at source, no matter how rich and extensive previous research might be, the link cannot be reverse-engineered.[3] However, because most companies have never researched customer values in any depth before, they do not have these links in place. Usually, therefore, they need to do new research, and this research needs to be designed very carefully. Marketers need to think through and anticipate every possible angle of analysis before they finalize the research details. Afterwards is too late.

It is all too easy, for example, to define 'the market' too narrowly and then to miss key differences between different aspects of the market: there is a big difference between researching the market for male wet shaving and the overall market for hair removal. Hair removal spans men and women, razors, shavers, and other hair-removing devices. To understand a wet shaving brand's real performance and

---

3 There are ways of creating approximations, but they are definitely second best.

How well original values research is designed is key to how much value and insight will be generated as a whole. If early connections are not made between data fields – such as brand values and age, or brand usage – then they cannot be 'reverse-engineered' into the data. This means marketers need to anticipate their future research needs, and build in flexibility, right from the start.

potential, marketers may well need to understand this broader market.

Other technicalities also need to be considered, such as the best definition of 'use.' Is a 'user' somebody who has purchased once over the last month? Or over the last year? To be a user do you have to buy the product regularly or just occasionally? Either way, we need to define 'regular' and 'occasional.' Such distinctions become important if marketers want to distinguish between 'heavy' and 'light' users of the category, especially for brands with large market penetrations.

MERGING VALUES ANALYSIS WITH TRADITIONAL TOOLS

Values analysis is not a replacement for traditional market research: it is an addition to the market research armory. And the resulting analyses can be designed to bring the different approaches together in an integrated way.

The brand conversion ladder, for example (see Figure 5.13), is a classic analytical tool using standard brand awareness and usage data to assess the brand's ability to turn awareness into sales, and to turn customers into brand advocates. An important theme here is assessing the brand's performance in recruiting both positive brand protagonists and antagonists. A high number of antagonists is not necessarily bad news. Sometimes, in order to win the strong and active commitment of one target group, the brand needs to create positive antipathy among another group: a pop and fashion brand might never be cool if 'My mum likes it.' Being hated by mum and dad may be a part of the brand's positive cachet among its target users.

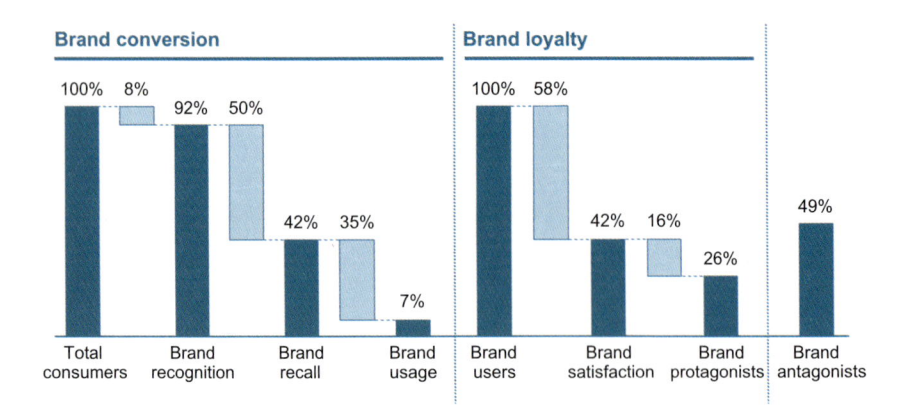

Figure 5.13 A brand conversion ladder
Source: Roland Berger Strategy Consultants

But how does such loyalty analysis fit with values profiling? Figure 5.14 shows one possibility. The chart analyzes the performance of the brand along two dimensions: 'Brand energy' and 'Brand mass.'

Brand energy shows how distinctive a brand is, and how well it targets its particular market. This score is gathered directly from values data: how well does this brand profile fit the market's drivers, and how distinctive is its brand profile (that is, how many contour lines does it show)? Brand mass is a score derived from the brand conversion ladder, showing how good the brand is at turning awareness into sales and loyalty.

The figure shows how brand energy and mass analysis can help brand managers assess their current position and future potential. Every brand in the market can be placed somewhere on this grid. Terms like 'eagles' and 'tigers' help dramatize different brands' positions.

◆ 'Eagles' are brands with high brand energy but low brand mass. They are highly differentiated in their markets and have a lot of 'thrust' in their brand. However, this thrust has not yet been turned into high sales or market penetration. Something needs to be done to capitalize on the brand's energy, to build its market momentum. If this is not happening, what's the obstacle?

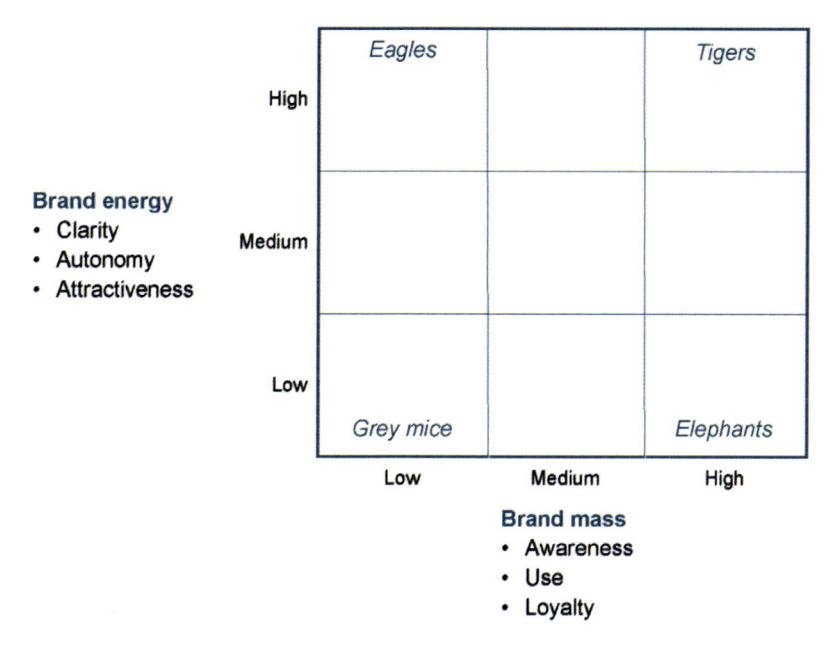

Figure 5.14 Brand mass/energy analysis
Source: Roland Berger Strategy Consultants

◆ 'Grey mice' lack both differentiation or 'energy,' and market mass or momentum. This is a graveyard for brands.

◆ 'Elephants' are big, apparently successful brands with large user bases and perhaps high market shares. But they no longer have a distinctive value proposition, and risk losing momentum rapidly should new, more attractive competitors appear on the scene.

◆ 'Tigers' are in the ideal position every brand manager dreams about: a big impact on the market in terms of brand awareness and sales, and a highly distinctive position, which means the brand still has plenty more energy.

Most brands start out small, with low market penetration, but they are very popular with a small group of enthusiasts. At this stage brand managers' prime focus is making the brand more distinctive: increasing its energy. Then, at a certain point, increased energy leads to increased mass: the brand grows more popular (awareness increases).

More people buy it more often. It becomes more widely distributed. At this point, brand managers' focus is on how best to turn popularity into growth.

The biggest challenges come next. The ideal, of course, is to be a 'tiger' with both high energy and high brand mass. In reality, however, few brands can achieve the ideal position. They face constraints and trade-offs as illustrated in Figure 5.15. Some may be able to push directly towards 'tiger' status, increasing both distinctiveness and market penetration. But this is rarely sustainable: it is very difficult to build brand energy and mass at the same time. Time and again, brands find a high-energy status leading to increased brand mass – but at the price of a loss of energy. Alternatively, they increase their energy at the cost of reduced mass (they become more sharply focused, thereby increasing their standing among core users, but lose others on the edges). Choosing which direction to follow is one of the key decisions in brand management.

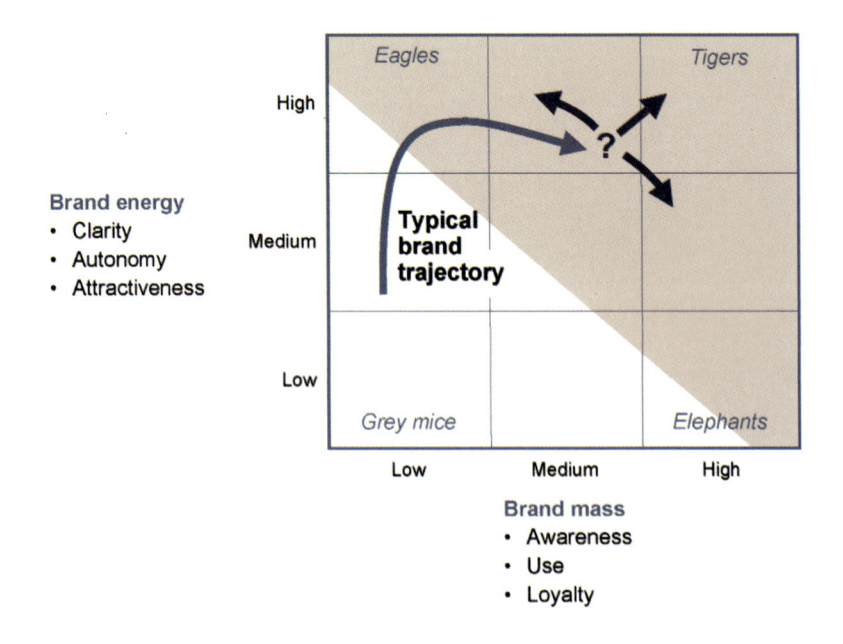

Figure 5.15 Assessing a brand's future direction
Source: Roland Berger Strategy Consultants

SUMMARY

There are countless ways to analyze brand performance and to identify potential ways forward for particular brands. In using the vast array of tools and techniques on the market, however, brand managers face two common problems. First, it's easy to become like a blind man groping the elephant – focusing too hard on just one aspect while missing the significance of others. Measuring brand performance solely in terms of brand awareness is useless if awareness is not being turned into sales. Measuring brand performance in terms of sales is useless if you have no insight into what is driving sales, and how to maintain and improve this performance. Successful brand management comes from the integration of many different viewpoints. We must have that Ariadne-thread.

The second common problem is that while some viewpoints are based on hard data, other viewpoints are often based on subjective assessment. It's hard to argue with sales data; it's quite easy to debate how successfully a brand is differentiating itself on the market.

Adding values-based analysis into the equation helps address both these problems. 'Hard' values data helps provide a common foundation for all analysis. It shows how the different parts of the elephant fit together. It also brings hard, factual evidence to areas commonly dominated by subjective opinions and intuition. And it provides marketers with the opportunity to 'slice and dice' this data from all manner of different angles in the search for insight.

Such brand diagnosis should have already raised a range of questions, such as:

◆ Is the brand appealing to values that are irrelevant to, or perhaps even put off, most market participants?

◆ Does the brand have a sharp, clear values profile, or is it more 'bland' than 'brand'?

◆ Are there any gaps in the market, as identified by customer segment analysis or joint space mapping?

◆ Is it good at turning brand recognition into sales into loyalty? Where does it miss the most value?

◆ Is the brand lacking energy or mass?

◆ Is it evolving in the right direction?

This chapter has outlined many such slicing/dicing insight-generating tools. The next step is to turn insight into strategy, by identifying alternative ways forward and assessing their relative merits.

6   From insight to brand strategy

Values-based brand management

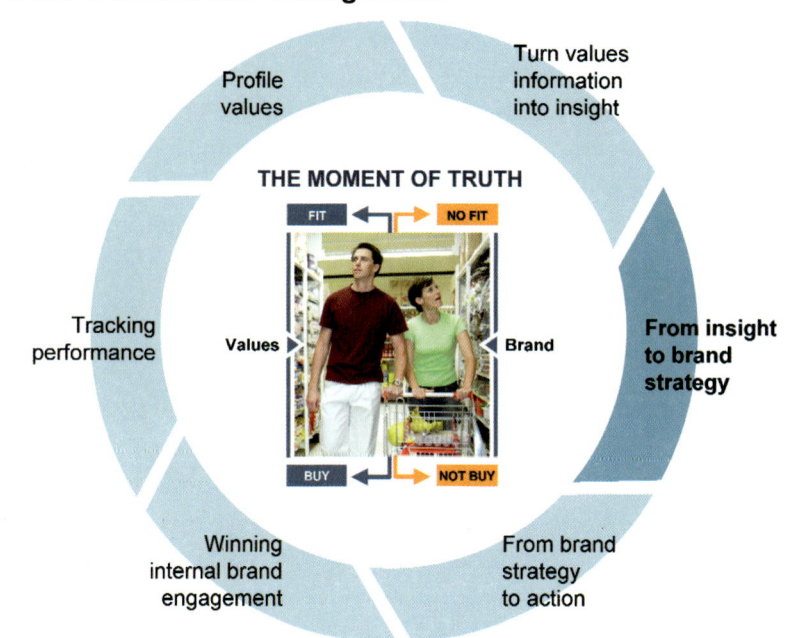

Roche Diagnostics is a division of the global pharmaceuticals giant Roche. With a turnover of 7.8 billion Swiss francs (2004 figures), Roche Diagnostics is a world leader in medical diagnostic equipment and reagents, with market shares commonly reaching over 50 percent. But a few years back, Roche faced a new challenge – a number of new challenges, in fact.

First, as a market leader Roche Diagnostics was continually under fire from hungry competitors willing to cut prices. Intensifying price competition was beginning to erode margins. Second, some of these competitors were winning for themselves a reputation for innovation, whereas Roche Diagnostics was renowned for other attributes such as high quality and reliability. This was beginning to worry Roche marketers: were they losing branch cachet? Third, growth in its traditional core diagnostics markets was slowing. Meanwhile the market itself was changing, with the introduction of new technologies: molecular, point-of-care, and DNA testing, for example.

Roche Diagnostics also faced a range of 'home grown' challenges. Its vast portfolio of products (tens of thousands of different stock-keeping units) had spawned a jungle of product brands with little internal coherence or logic. Yet its technical, scientifically oriented workforce did not believe better brand management was a priority. So how was Roche Diagnostics to defend its market leader status (and profitability), and evolve its brands and offerings with the times, while simultaneously streamlining and improving the effectiveness of its marketing operations?

With 4000 hotels in 140 countries, **Accor** is one of the biggest hotel groups in the world and market leader in Europe. In 2002, as part of its expansion, it became a major shareholder in the largest German hotel chain, Dorint Hotels & Resorts. The two companies wanted to create a brand win–win.

In Germany, the Dorint brand was perceived as being stronger all round. Accor wanted to improve the standing of some of its own brands, such as Sofitel, Novotel, and Mercure, by associating them with Dorint via co-branding. Dorint wanted better access to international markets, where the Accor brands were very strong overall.

Creating such a win–win would be difficult, however. The Dorint and Accor brands were perceived differently and attracted different consumer segments. It would not be easy to appeal to these different segments under one co-brand umbrella without losing customers. How could Accor integrate Dorint into its existing portfolio in a way that strengthened the overall portfolio: so that it covered the market as a whole, without overlapping positionings appealing to the same target groups or causing confusion in the marketplace?

This challenge was compounded by the Accor and Dorint brands' markedly different histories and strategies. Accor's strategy had been to develop one brand for every category. It had different brands for different price points, ranging from one-star economy hotels to top-of-the range five-star luxury. The Dorint strategy on the other hand had been to create one strong brand for all categories, with clear star ratings from three-star to five-star to distinguish different categories, rather like BMW with its Series 7, 5, and 3. Thus the two brand strategies were contradictory.

PUTTING DATA TO WORK

Stories such as these are the meat and drink of brand strategy. Marketers add value to their organizations by finding a way through the dilemmas created by such peculiarities of history, geography, market, and people. It's what the day job is all about: how do we cope with changing market conditions, pressure from new competitors, or sagging growth and margins? How do we handle mergers and acquisitions? How do we manage brand portfolios?

Over the past four chapters we have shown how a values-based approach can cast new light on such dilemmas and illuminate new possibilities by:

◆ analyzing the values of the people who participate in the market (as opposed to those who don't) to identify the values driving the market

◆ analyzing the values of the people who buy a brand, as opposed to those who don't, to identify weaknesses and opportunities

◆ comparing a brand's profile with those of the market as whole, with other brands, and with specific customer segments including values archetypes

◆ mapping competing brands on a values map to show which brands appeal most to which archetypes, and to help identify gaps in the market

◆ drilling down into detail, for example, to analyze the values of particular customer segments (by age, income, and so on), comparing these with market drivers, brand profiles, and archetypes.

We have analyzed. We have diagnosed. Using our Ariadne-thread of values-based analysis we have worked our way to the heart of the marketing maze. Now we need to find our way out, to use what we have learnt to formulate strategy.

In a values-based approach, the heart of effective strategy formulation is conceptually very simple. First, identify which values segments are the most economically attractive (or, if you already know which consumers are most economically attractive, identify their values). Second, identify what the brand needs to do in terms of both rational and emotional attributes to appeal to these most economically attractive segments. And third, test the proposed brand positioning against the brand/organization's ability to achieve it. (In some cases, the 'ideal' brand positioning is simply too far away from current market perceptions of the brand and/or the organization's ability to deliver the proposed brand promise.)

To do this, we need to bring every bit of information we can to bear on the problem. This is where the design of our original research is put to the test. Ideally, our earlier research has not only identified the values of category users (market drivers) and of our brand and our competitors (actual value propositions), it has also teased out market shares, purchase frequencies and volumes, customer demographics (including age, gender, marital status, monthly income, region, and so on), product usage habits, perceptions of the brand and its competitors on key areas of value, shopping, and media consumption habits, and so on. (See Figure 6.1.) Using this data, we will also have a good idea of the 'personalities' of our most important customers: a picture of them, their likes and dislikes, attitudes towards life and society, and so on.

Because this research has been done with values in mind, every data field can be linked back to values and sliced and diced to tease out the particular attributes of different values groups. It is our Ariadne-thread. This data can then be used in a number of ways:

◆ to analyze the economic attractiveness of different archetypes or values groups

◆ to analyze how good the brand is at attracting these most economically attractive archetypes or groups (customer base analysis and brand signatures)

◆ to map all competitor brands according to how well they attract various archetypes, thereby identifying potential gaps in the market (joint space analysis)

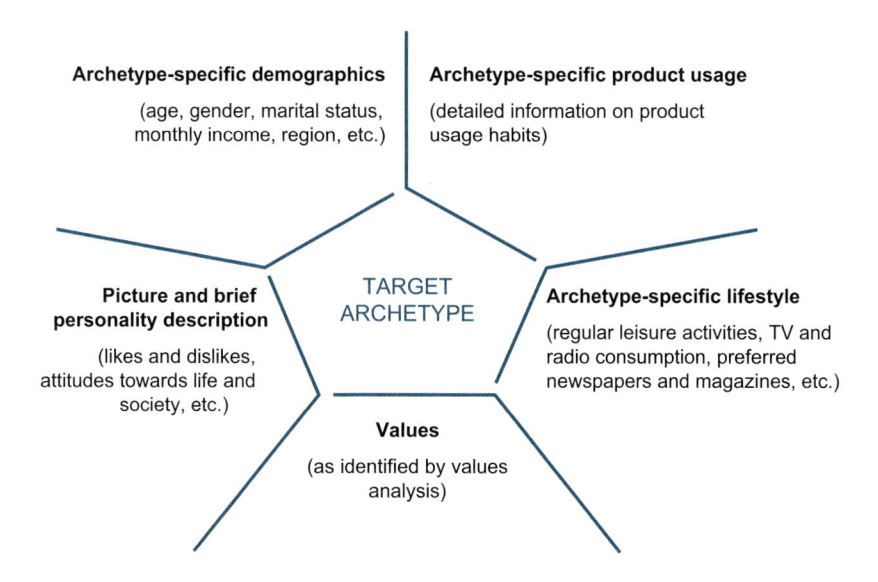

Figure 6.1 Integrated data sources drive seamless, detailed implementation
Source: Roland Berger Strategy Consultants

◆ to develop alternative target value propositions which highlight the values the brand intends to appeal to and to distance itself from

◆ to assess the relative economic benefits of these different alternatives while judging how easy/expensive it will be to achieve them, and in this way to identify which alternative to pursue (brand strategy scorecards).

The rest of this chapter outlines how these tools work, and provides some examples of the different applications they can be used for.

The tools outlined in this chapter are part of a complete strategic brand management toolkit. They are not designed to fit every circumstance. It is not a methodological requirement that every tool is used on every occasion. The tools are simply there to be used when and where they can help get the job done.

ANALYZING ECONOMIC ATTRACTIVENESS

One of the core assumptions of values analysis is that some brands attract people with a certain set of values, while other brands attract people with different values. Having clustered people of similar values together, we can then see which clusters spend more on the category and the brand, what their potential spending power is, and how likely they are to spend given their values. Figure 6.2 represents a simple analysis of the economic attractiveness of different German consumer archetypes, related to the consumer electronics category.

The methodology is very simple: just rank each archetype by different criteria. Nevertheless it does tease out the key considerations for marketers. The biggest segment, in this case Performers, might not be the biggest users of the category (marked 'consumption' in the figure). Or the category's values profile might mean it does not appeal to Performers. In this case, for example, the fifth largest

Consumer electronics, Germany

	% of total population	Rank of total population	Category affinity	Con-sumption	Overall rank
Top priority[1]					
Performers	18.5	1	2	2	1
Maximalists	13.9	3	3	1	2
Medium relevance[1]					
Hedonists	9.3	5	1	6	3
Individualists	7.9	8	4	4	4
Out of scope[1]					
Dreamers	12.5	4	5	3	5
Humanists	16.5	2	7	7	6
Traditionalists	8.4	7	8	5	7
Minimalists	8.8	6	6	8	8

1) Grouping according to strategic / economic relevance

Figure 6.2 Analyzing the economic attractiveness of different consumer archetypes
Source: Roland Berger Strategy Consultants, TNS data
(Germany, March 2002, n=1500, population 14–65 years, CATI)

segment – the Individualists – has the closest affinity to the category, and the third largest category is actually the biggest spender overall. It is the combination of these factors that gives the final ranking of economic attractiveness.

Figure 6.2 is a relatively simple example of the analysis that can be brought to bear. Figure 6.3 shows a more detailed economic attractiveness analysis undertaken by a Chinese sports shoe and apparel brand. Each archetype's size is broken down into big cities, second and third-tier cities and overall (remember the archetypes are different from those in Figure 6.2 because they are Chinese rather than German). Consumption has been ranked by both personal and family income. How much the archetypes spend on sports shoes and sports apparel generally has been ranked, as well as how active they are as users of shoes and apparel. Taking all such factors into account, the relative attractiveness of each archetype has been assessed.

Chinese archetypes in order of economic relevance

Chinese Archetypes	Economic Relevance	Size (%) Overall	Big cities	Tier 2–3 cities	Consumption Personal/ Family Income	Spending Index	Affinity sports (%) Sport pursuit	Spending shoes	Spending wear	Sub-market driver
Progressive Maximalists	1	10	11	9	2.656 (1)	Very high	+8	392 (1)	427 (1)	'Luxury'
Traditional Maximalists	2	14	14	14	2.587 (2)	Very high	+7	287 (2)	329 (3)	24
Self-centered	3	21	24	18	2.338 (4)	Low	-1	279 (3)	342 (2)	'Non-conformist'
Hedonists	4	14	14	13	2.142 (6)	Medium	+4	264 (4)	303 (4)	35
Modern Performers	5	13	11	14	2.377 (3)	Low	-3	234 (5)	262 (6)	'Performance'
Traditionalists	6	10	8	14	2.319 (5)	Medium	-4	214 (6)	265 (5)	23
Conformists	7	12	13	11	1.945 (7)	Very low	-6	197 (7)	228 (7)	'Price'
Minimalists	8	6	5	6	1.657 (8)	Very low	-11	164 (8)	166 (8)	18

Figure 6.3 Digging deeper into the economic attractiveness of different archetypes (sports apparel, China)
Source: Roland Berger Strategy Consultants, TNS data
(China, August 2004, n=4950, population 12–65 years, CATI)

CUSTOMER BASE ANALYSIS

Once we have an idea of the attractiveness of archetypes generally, we need to know how good the brand is at attracting these archetypes. This involves breaking the brand's own customer base down by archetype. A brand that is unable to attract any particular archetype will find that the profile of brand buyers reflects that of the population as a whole. A brand that is very good at attracting some archetypes will boast proportionately more of these archetypes, and therefore proportionately less of others.

A 'good' brand signature, therefore, shows two things. First, it shows a high degree of representation among the most economically attractive archetypes. Second, the archetypes it is successful with have similar values. If, say, the two most economically attractive archetypes have very different values, it will be difficult for the brand to target them both. So there is a constant trade-off between economic relevance and clear brand identity/targeting.

One way of representing a good brand signature is illustrated in Figure 6.4. The archetypes are listed from top to bottom in order of decreasing economic relevance: the brand has a much

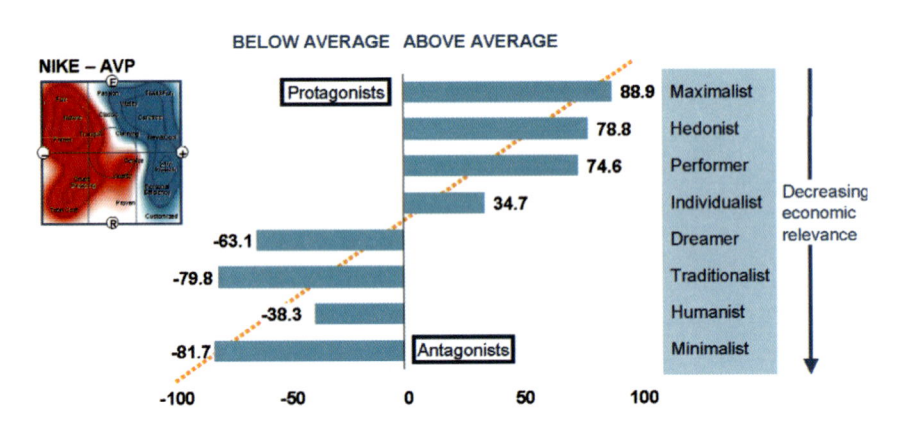

Consumer base analysis (deviation from sample population in %)

Figure 6.4 A 'good' brand signature (Nike, Germany 2002)
Source: Roland Berger Strategy Consultants, Emnid data
(Germany, March 2002, n=1500, population 14–65 years, CATI)

higher representation among the attractive archetypes on the top (the Maximalists and Hedonists, for example) and much lower representation among the least attractive archetypes such as the Minimalists. The sloping diagonal line is the signature of a brand with a strong profile.

By the way, not all signatures need to look the same. Figure 6.5 shows an equally successful brand with an equally 'good' signature: the German hard discounter Aldi. This time the strong diagonal line slopes in the other direction. Here the most economically attractive archetype is the Minimalists on the bottom, followed by the Humanists and Traditionalists.

For each brand, then, the most economically attractive archetypes will be different, so each brand signature will be different. Often, however, the brand's actual penetration of the different archetypes does not follow this neat slope from the most economically attractive to the least. Figure 6.6 for example, shows a 'weak' brand signature. Here, the brand is extremely 'democratized' (attracting no values group in particular). The dotted line shows the ideal signature, the bars show the actual. We return to the dilemmas of democratized brands in Chapter 9.

Consumer base analysis (deviation from sample population in %)

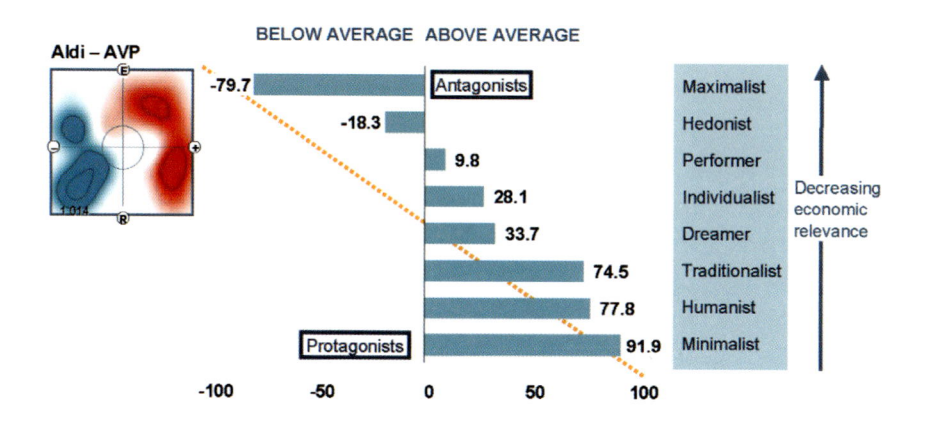

Figure 6.5 Another 'good' brand signature (Aldi, Germany 2002)
Source: Roland Berger Strategy Consultants, Emnid data
(Germany, March 2002, n=1500, population 14–65 years, CATI)

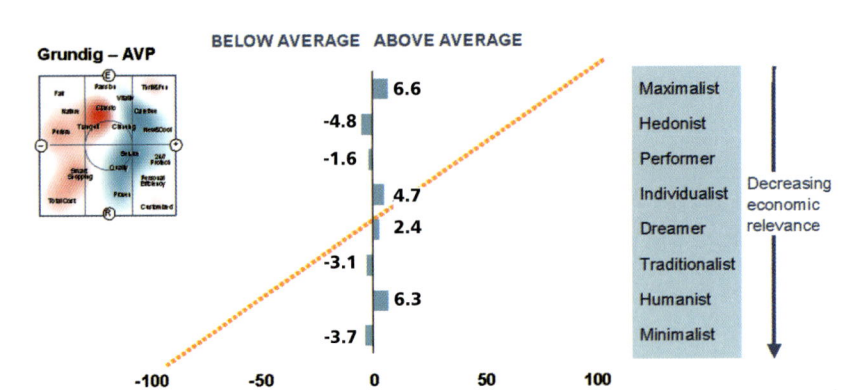

Consumer base analysis (deviation from sample population in %)

Figure 6.6 A 'weak' brand signature (Grundig, Germany 2002)
Source: Roland Berger Strategy Consultants, Emnid data
(Germany, March 2002, n=1500, population 14–65 years, CATI)

JOINT SPACE ANALYSIS

A common next step is to conduct a joint space analysis to show, visually, which archetypes all the main brands are best at attracting. This introduces the competitor element into the equation (perhaps the most economically attractive segment is already 'sewn up' by a rival brand), and it helps highlight potential market gaps. Figure 6.7 shows the result of a joint space analysis conducted by the vertical fashion retailer Esprit in Germany.

The joint space analysis places every relevant brand on the map according to how good it is at attracting each particular archetype. A brand that is purchased only by one archetype would be placed 'on top' of that archetype. (These archetypes may be representative of the population generally, or more specifically researched archetypes representing specific values segments within the overall population of category users.)

A brand that is purchased equally by two archetypes (but by no others) would be placed equally between those two archetypes. A

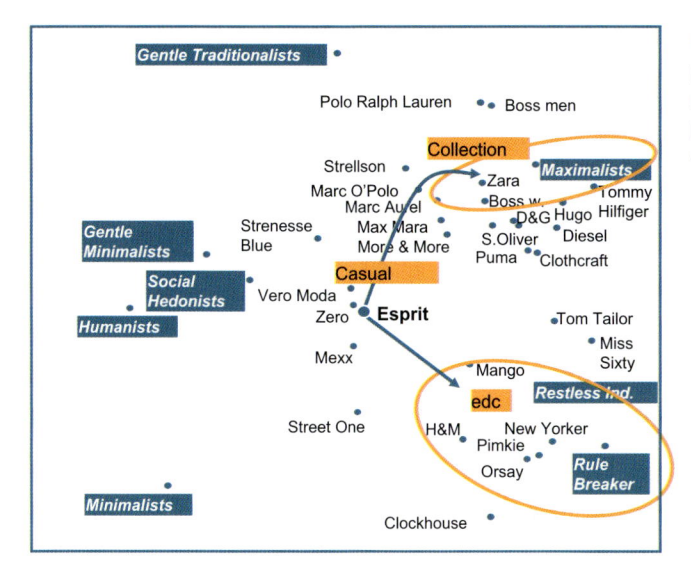

Esprit's original position vis-à-vis rival brands, and possible brand extensions

Figure 6.7 A joint space analysis showing possible brand or sub-brand trajectories
Source: Roland Berger Strategy Consultants, Roland Berger Market Research data (Germany, May 2003, n=715, population 14–50 years, CATI)

brand that is purchased equally by all archetypes would be placed in the middle, equidistant from them all. In this particular analysis, the resulting map showed Esprit that it had opportunities in two directions. The main brand was positioned successfully in the middle, but there were significant clusters of brands gravitating towards the economically attractive Maximalists in the north-east corner and the Individualists and Rule breakers in the south-east corner. (The Minimalists in the extreme south-western corner are not active in this market, which explains why there are no brands addressing them.)

Moving the main brand would have involved too great a sacrifice of existing strengths and market share. However, by launching specific sub-brands aimed at these very different market segments, Esprit would be able to develop a three-pronged strategy to extend its market presence. It did this through the development of Esprit Collection (a distinctive concept with a high fashion and quality claim), the edc sub-brand for the Rule breaker and Restless individualist segments, plus a refreshed, revitalized position for Esprit Casual.

We will return to joint space analysis in Chapter 9 when we discuss the role of values and archetypes in innovation.

Sharp-eyed readers will notice that the names given to the various archetypes, and their positioning on the map, are different from those on the joint space map first shown in Chapter 4. The reason for this is simple. The map in Chapter 4 depicts archetypes from the entire population. In this research however, Esprit focused only on 14–50-year-olds – its target market. It then identified the most distinctive clusters within this population and gave them its own names, such as 'Gentle hedonist' and 'Rule breaker,' to describe them.

So far, we have assessed the relative economic attractiveness of different archetypes or values groups, analyzed the brand's success (or failure) in attracting the most attractive archetypes, and then compared the brand's position to that of competitors. This joint space analysis highlights opportunities for the brand to go 'south,' 'east,' or 'west' – wherever it needs to go to win over the most economically attractive customer segments. We are now in a position to develop target value propositions.

TARGET VALUE PROPOSITIONS

A target value proposition (TVP) represents the combination of values that the brand needs to address – and distance itself from – if it is going to be successful in attracting its targeted customer segment. Figure 6.8 shows the TVP of a European telecoms provider. The 'backbone' of the brand is built around five core values – Vitality, Clanning, Carefree, Service, and Quality. This backbone is shown by the blue lines in the main chart in Figure 6.8 and also by the white lines on the archetype profiles. This demonstrates a key element of the art of TVP development. Previous research for this brand had identified Progressive performers as the most attractive archetype. Meanwhile the brand was already particularly strong with the Traditionalists and Traditionalist maximalists. The five backbone values are common to all three. By focusing on these values, the brand will be able to strengthen its position with its current core customers while also attracting more of the most economically attractive segment.

But the TVP does not consist solely of the big blue dots of the brand backbone. It is also supplemented by another positive value: Proven,

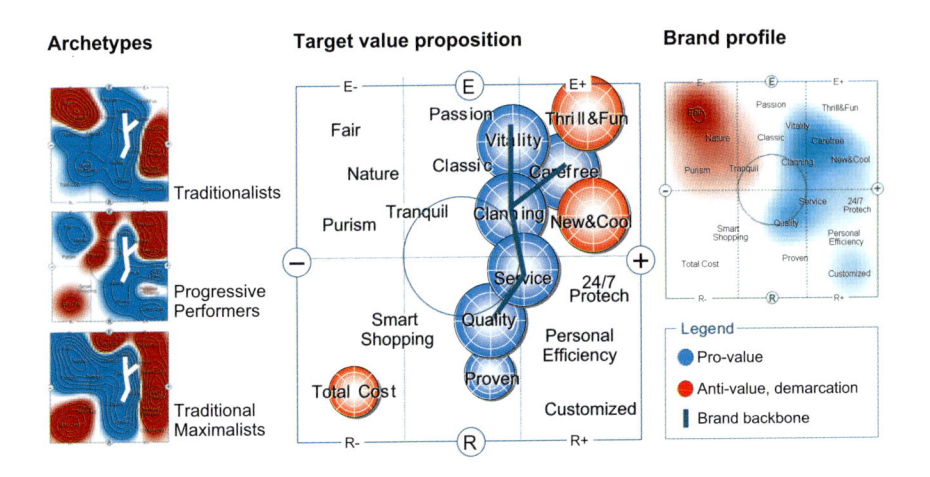

Figure 6.8 A target value proposition compared with key archetypes
Source: Roland Berger Strategy Consultants

as shown by the smaller blue dot. This should also be pursued by the brand, though with less emphasis than the 'backbone' values. We will see later how adding 'sub-values' like this can help to develop sub-brand and umbrella brand strategies, where the umbrella brand focuses on the backbone values, and sub-brands emphasize additional sub-values.

The TVP is also complemented by highly specific 'anti-values,' shown in red. In brand-building terms, such 'anti-values' can be just as important as positive values because they underline what the brand is *not*: a brand that is not 'anti' anything runs a great risk of appearing bland. Anti-values therefore need to be chosen just as carefully as positive values. In this case, all three target archetypes are positive rejectors of New and cool. Two of them also reject Thrill and fun and Total cost, while the third archetype is neutral (it doesn't really care either way). It is therefore safe for the brand to choose these anti-values: it won't turn any of its target archetypes off.

However, choosing a robust TVP does not involve simply looking at a few pretty pictures and identifying some common red or blue dots. That is just the first step: identifying alternatives. Subsequently each of these alternatives needs to be assessed – by building a comprehensive economic model of how the brand currently earns its money from which customer segments; how adopting the new TVP will attract some and put off others, and how this translates into increased or reduced revenues; and the cost of making the changes. This is not a matter of licking a finger and sticking it in the air. It depends absolutely on the ability to combine deep understanding of the business's internal economics and dynamics with the insights generated from the values-based research.

Figure 6.9 outlines the sort of methodology that needs to be used in such analysis. The top left-hand part of the analysis identifies the number and value of customers likely to be gained and lost as a result of the shift to the new TVP. The customer base is broken down into three groups: OU standing for occasional users, FU for frequent users and IU for intensive users. It shows that while the new brand proposition alienates some existing customers, overall it adds more revenue than is lost.

The top right-hand part of the chart identifies how these changes are to be achieved, over time. Not all the gains will be made in the first

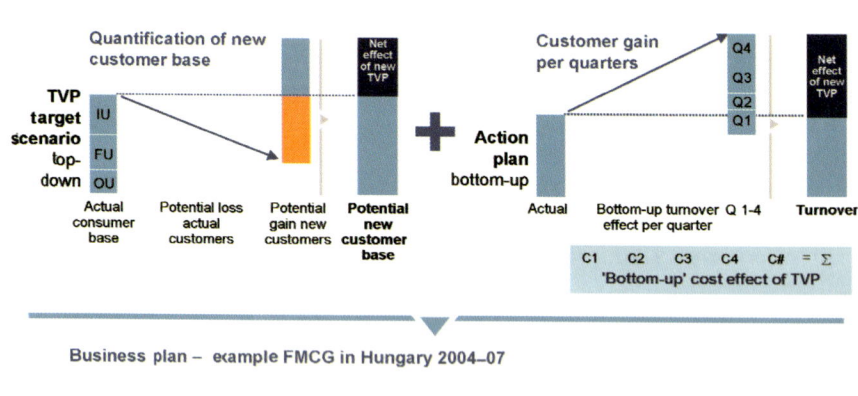

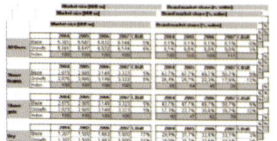

Figure 6.9 Identifying the potential economic impact of alternative brand strategies: key steps
Source: Roland Berger Strategy Consultants

quarter: they will accumulate as the new brand proposition beds down in the marketplace and as the company brings in all the actions necessary to make it a reality. The bottom side of the chart shows how these projections work their way through the usual business variables such as turnover, costs of goods, and overhead.

We are now ready for the final step: choosing which option to go for.

BRAND STRATEGY SCORECARDS

The number crunching involved in assessing the economic implications of alternative brand strategies may be complex, but ultimately the final decision should be made as clear and simple as possible. Again, if it is possible to visualize the key factors, the chances of triggering a sound discussion and reaching a commonly understood, considered judgment are greater.

Figure 6.10 depicts a simple brand strategy scorecard, which assesses five alternative strategies identified from a joint space analysis. The analysis suggested that the brand could migrate in one of five directions

Brand strategy scorecard

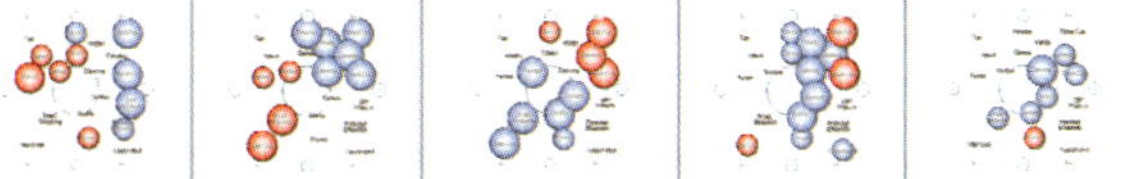

		'Go east'	'Go south'	'Go north-west'	'Go west'	'Go north-east'
Brand positioning	Clarity	6	8	8	8	5
	Uniqueness	5	5	7	9	6
Economic potential	Market share change	1	5	5	10	0
	Value share change	1	5	4	10	0
	Summary assessment	3	6	5	9	2
	Ability to execute[2]	✔	?	?	✔	✘

[1] Scores indicate the degree of fulfillment. 0 indicates no fulfillment at all and 10 indicates complete possible fulfillment
[2] Roland Berger assessment   ✔ Given   ? Uncertain   ✘ Difficult

Figure 6.10 Assessing the value and risk of alternative brand strategies
Source: Roland Berger Strategy Consultants

(east, north-east, and so on), and the economic implications of each journey were assessed.

Further considerations were added. How clear and unique would the new brand positioning be? Which is the clearest, most differentiated choice of all the options? Combined with the economic assessment (such as market share and margin implications), each alternative course is given a summary assessment.

In this case, the conclusion is relatively straightforward. 'Go east' is one of the easiest options – it involves the least change from the current status quo. But at the same time, the economic analysis also shows it delivers the least benefit in market share or value share (apart from 'Go north-east' which offers no economic benefit at all).

Finally, one more step is needed: the 'filter' consideration of whether or not the company is indeed able to implement this strategy. In this case, 'Go south' and 'Go north-west' offer great value and market share gains – and greater brand differentiation and clarity – but they have a crucial drawback. They involve significant movement away from the brand's current strengths. The risks of such a shift, plus doubts about the company's ability to execute such a radical change, put a question mark over these alternatives. Building as it does on current perceptions of the brand (even though weakly held), 'Go west' goes with the grain of the market while also offering the greatest potential economic benefits. Now, all its marketers have to do is implement the strategy, consistently, in everything they do!

Now, having assessed the main steps in the strategy formulation process, let's see how they were applied in the cases of Accor and Roche Diagnostics as introduced at the beginning of this chapter.

CASE STUDY: ACCOR

The first thing Accor did was to research the values of hotel users, which turned out to be slightly different from those of the population as whole: nine, rather than eight, values archetypes were identified. Its next step was to analyze the economic attractiveness of each of these archetypes: how often they stay and how much they spend on hotels; whether this is for leisure or business purposes; their market size and booking behavior (through for example a travel agent, a secretary, or the Internet), and how wealthy they are. In this way, Accor could create a 'single view' of each archetype: what brand attributes it is most attracted to, and what value it represents to the company. Figure 6.11 summarizes the results for one such archetype, 'Conservative maximalists.'

This gave Accor the basis for assessing each archetype's potential economic value, taking account of the size of the segment, what it used hotels for (business or leisure), and so on. Four of the nine archetypes emerged as simply not economically attractive (they did not use hotels very often). The picture of the other five was more mixed.

For example, one of the smallest segments was 'Performers,' who focus very clearly on rational benefits such as technology and efficiency, and are positively put off by values such as Thrill and fun and New and cool. However, even though their numbers were relatively small, they were very frequent hotel users, mainly for business reasons, with above-average income.

Accor also analyzed the values profile of various brands within its portfolio. This exposed some sharp differences between brands. For example, one of its brands had more than double its 'fair share' of

Conservative Maximalist
consumer segment

zmax = 12.7   n = 79 vs. 1,419
hc = 98 vs. 1,403

Overall

Average age:	39 years
Market size (20–65):	8.1%
Ø Household net income p.m.:	3,658 EUR
Ø No. of nights in hotels p.y.:	11.4
Share of business/leisure customers:	49% / 51%
Share of business/leisure nights:	65% / 35%

Characteristics

- Traditional performance orientations play an important role in his/her life
- Sets high standards on security and reliability as well as on quality and service
- High affinity towards new technologies and innovations
- Need to make the best out of his/her time (quickness, efficiency), looking for individual solutions
- Demand for materialistic things and desire for status symbols
- Anti-minimalist – likes to spend money and enjoy life
- Friendship and social acceptance are important – but not welfare-oriented

Figure 6.11 Analyzing archetypes' economic attractiveness, hotel example
Source: Roland Berger Strategy Consultants, TNS Emnid data
(Germany, September 2003, n=1500, population 14–65 years, CATI)

Performers, while being considerably under-represented by another archetype – the Humanists. Another one of its brands had an almost opposite profile – particularly low take-up by Performers and particularly high take-up among Humanists.

With this insight into the values of hotel users generally, the market drivers of the hotel industry (in other words, the values of hotel users generally), and the customers of each hotel brand, Accor was now able to develop a coherent brand strategy, with each brand targeting a particular archetype. In this way, it could cover most of the market with its portfolio brands while avoiding cannibalism between them. Each brand would have its own clear and differentiated positioning. And each brand would contribute to the strength of the portfolio as a whole. Thus the analysis could be used to 'kill two birds with one stone': create a clearer positioning for each brand *and* a more coherent brand architecture.

Figure 6.12 illustrates the core outcome. With its strong focus on the performance values of Personal efficiency and 24/7 pro-tech, with a touch of New and cool and Customized, the Dorint-Novotel brand

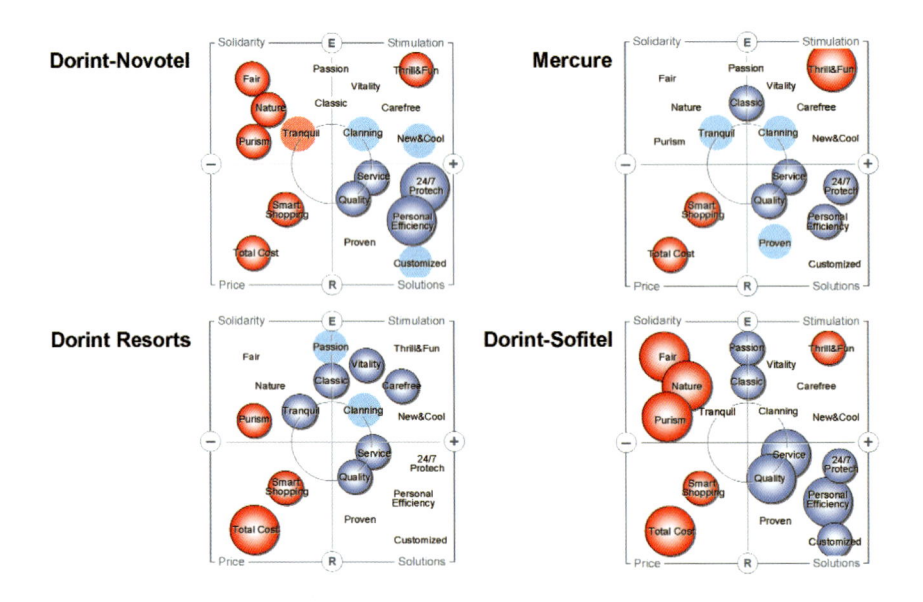

Figure 6.12 The different target value propositions compared
Source: Roland Berger Strategy Consultants

would be positioned as the modern, contemporary and functional four-star hotel, clearly focused on the business traveler market. Its target archetype was the Performer. To emphasize personal efficiency, for example, it would introduce automated check-outs and car hire facilities in every hotel. To emphasize 24/7 pro-tech it would make wireless LANs available in every hotel along with top-class conference facilities with 24-hour food and beverage offering.

The Mercure brand would be focused on the business market as well as on the leisure market, therefore it would address slightly more emotional values alongside the rational values for business. It would still address market drivers like Personal efficiency and 24/7 pro-tech, but do so with less emphasis, giving equal weight to other values such as Classic on the emotional side, with a touch of Tranquil and Clanning. It's a much more laid-back brand, which is much more appealing to Liberal traditionalists. Translated into a regional approach in décor and service, these hotels would create a respectable, traditional atmosphere, with a less standardized and hence more personal touch – giving the feeling that they act as gateways to their cities. At the same time, however, they would have modern technology and useful information for guests via the hotel television. But nothing over the top: New and cool and Customized don't figure here at all.

For the Dorint Leisure brand (renamed as Resort & Spa), 24/7 pro-tech and Personal efficiency don't figure at all, but Service, Quality, Vitality, Carefree, and Tranquil are important: this is clearly a leisure brand appealing to the Social reliable archetype. It would include sports facilities such as gyms and swimming pools, areas for wellness, relaxation, and repose, high-quality food, late checkout facilities (to emphasize a carefree appeal), and things like hotel bicycle rental – bringing service and vitality together.

Finally, for the Dorint-Sofitel five-star brand, Quality and Service loom large. The 24/7 pro-tech features represent the business needs. Personal efficiency and Customized also figure: these are luxury hotels delivering immediate special, personal service. Passion and Classic are also core values to attract the leisure guest. All the values would translate into especially experienced and knowledgeable concierge staff, fine art on the walls, fine wines in the restaurants, and a décor suggesting timeless elegance, with real fires, live piano in the reception area, a library, and so on. For the business guest, now-standard well-equipped conference rooms would be complemented by a boardroom with the latest technology, catering for high-end meetings. This brand would fit the Conservative maximalist profile (shown above) for luxury business and leisure almost perfectly.

Of course, there is some small overlap. Figure 6.13 shows a detailed analysis of the likely effects of the Dorint-Novotel's new TVP: how good (or bad) it would be at attracting different archetypes. For Performers, its appeal is spot on. But its emphasis on values such as 24/7 pro-tech, Personal efficiency, Quality, and Service means it also holds some attraction for other archetypes such as Conservative maximalists, Progressive hedonists, and Liberal traditionalists – they all have 'blue areas' in common.

Figure 6.14 collates such an analysis of each brand's appeal to show how, together, the brands collectively work together to cover the whole market.

With a new brand architecture in place, Accor was in a position to drill down into the detail of what each new TVP meant: for target

Brand attractiveness by customer segment: focused market 20–65 years

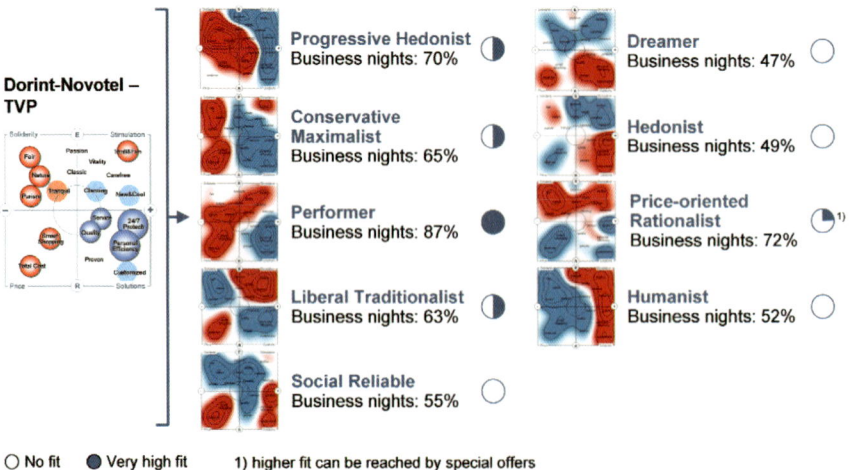

○ No fit   ● Very high fit   1) higher fit can be reached by special offers

Figure 6.13 Reviewing a brand's appeal to different archetypes
Source: Roland Berger Strategy Consultants, TNS Emnid data
(Germany, September 2003, n=1500, population 14–65 years, CATI)

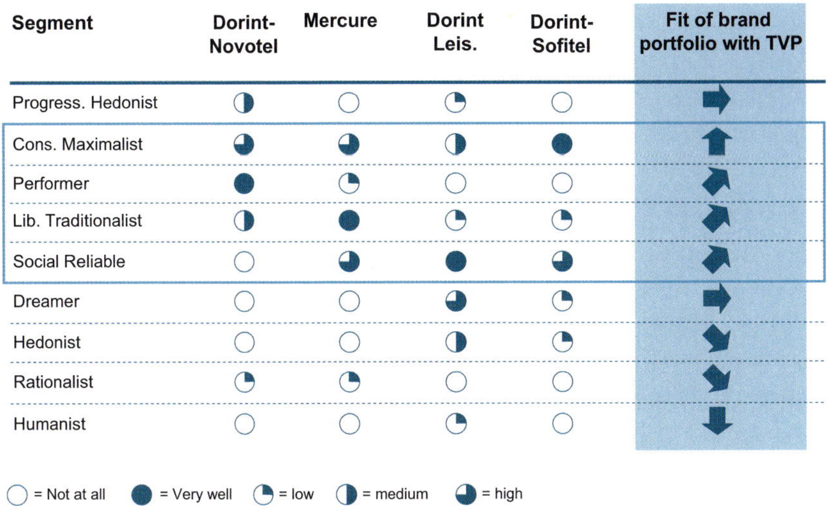

Segment	Dorint-Novotel	Mercure	Dorint Leis.	Dorint-Sofitel	Fit of brand portfolio with TVP
Progress. Hedonist	medium	Not at all	low	Not at all	→
Cons. Maximalist	high	high	medium	Very well	↑
Performer	Very well	low	Not at all	Not at all	↗
Lib. Traditionalist	medium	Very well	low	low	↗
Social Reliable	Not at all	high	Very well	high	↗
Dreamer	Not at all	Not at all	high	low	→
Hedonist	Not at all	Not at all	medium	low	↘
Rationalist	low	low	Not at all	Not at all	↘
Humanist	Not at all	Not at all	low	Not at all	↓

○ = Not at all   ● = Very well   ◔ = low   ◑ = medium   ◕ = high

Figure 6.14 Reviewing a brand portfolio's appeal to key market segments
Source: Roland Berger Strategy Consultants

market, hotel décor, services and facilities, type and style of food offered, marketing and advertising imagery, communication messages and sales presentations, distribution channels, and so on. We return to this – turning strategy into actions – in the next chapter.

CASE STUDY: ROCHE DIAGNOSTICS

In the case of Esprit, the core issue was brand positioning. For Accor the key issue was brand portfolio management. At Roche Diagnostics what started out as a brand positioning project became a brand portfolio exercise too – as values-based analysis opened marketers' eyes to new opportunities.

Roche Diagnostics was already highly successful, but its marketing options were constrained by a number of factors. Roche Diagnostics didn't have the luxury to choose which segment to target, for example: its target markets were already clearly defined for it. 'Near-patient' blood tests were used by physicians and intensive care units; 'centralized' diagnostic equipment was used mainly by large private and hospital laboratories; there were specialist users of new high-tech molecular equipment, and so on.

These different markets were addressed by separate business areas, and Roche Diagnostics already knew a lot about them. Roche marketers knew, for example, how well the equipment performed across a range of performance factors (reliability, accuracy, maintenance, and so on); price perceptions; whether customers felt they were under-serviced or over-serviced, and so on. But what Roche Diagnostics didn't know was its customers' values. So it researched the values of all decision makers and influencers – doctors, laboratory assistants, heads of departments, laboratory owners, and other groups. And, in an innovative step, it created a weighted average of their values profiles to reflect the different peoples' different degrees of purchasing influence (laboratory assistants versus department heads, for example).

Roche Diagnostics was stunned by the results. In technical and buyer terms it was clearly serving three distinct markets (hence the need for three distinct business areas). But the values profile of decision makers and influencers across all three markets was strikingly similar. They all embraced values such as Proven and Quality, and positively rejected values favoring innovation. What's more, this values profile was similar among customers across the world. Previously Roche marketers had simply assumed that three different businesses offering three different sets of products for three different markets needed three different brands. Now a new possibility had emerged: a single global brand embracing all three business areas.

Figure 6.15 illustrates the top-line results of this massive global research project. A new umbrella brand would be created (actually, an existing brand name – cobas® – researched as being the most appropriate), and it would focus on four core values: the three positives of Quality, Proven, and Clanning, plus the anti-value of Total cost (or 'Premium value').

These four core values would then be supplemented by extra values for sub-brands targeting specific markets (see Figure 6.16).

First, a sub-brand for the Roche Diagnostics' traditional B2B trade with laboratories was developed. This included the supplementary values of 'Confidence,' 'Customer focus,' and 'Innovation.' Sharp-eyed

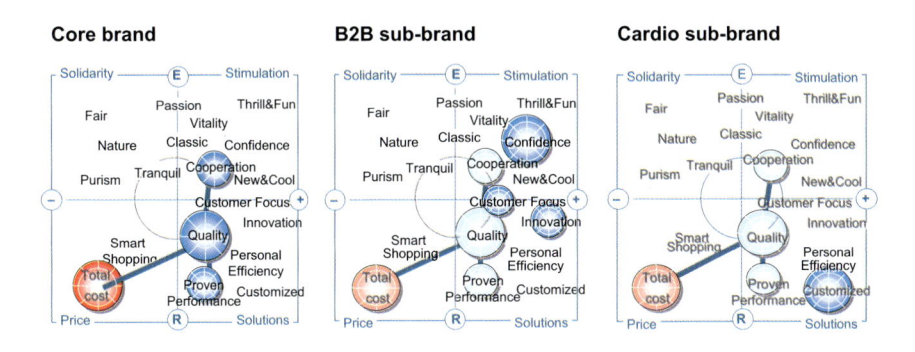

Actual value proposition

Values of existing customers

Target value proposition

Core values of the future brand

Figure 6.15 Developing Roche Diagnostics cobas's core value proposition
Source: Roche Diagnostics

readers will notice that these are not the values we usually talk about: they are how Roche Diagnostics interpreted and decided to communicate values we have previously discussed as Carefree, Service, and 24/7 pro-tech. Roche marketers also renamed 'Clanning' as 'Cooperation' – a concept its B2B partners and sales force would instantly recognize and approve of.

Core brand

B2B sub-brand

Cardio sub-brand

Figure 6.16 Building sub-brands on the core brand's total value proposition
Source: Roland Berger Strategy Consultants

Figure 6.17 shows how these target values were then interpreted for the division's particular customer base. Please note how the values are to be expressed through the brand's personality as a whole, and through both the rational and emotional supports which are designed to work together in a seamless, mutually reinforcing way.

Likewise, Roche Diagnostics developed an additional sub-brand for its cardio products (one of a range of indication-specific sub-brands to target physicians). It was intended to trigger increased demand for diagnostic testing by doctors and to a certain extent patients directly, using these sub-brand devices. Previous analysis had revealed that patients with different conditions expressed different values. For example, cardiology patients were extremely anti-innovation in their outlook: patient literature emphasizing the hi-tech devices that would be used to treat them was a positive turn-off. On the other hand, every heart condition (and patient) is different in some way: patients and doctors stressed the need for each

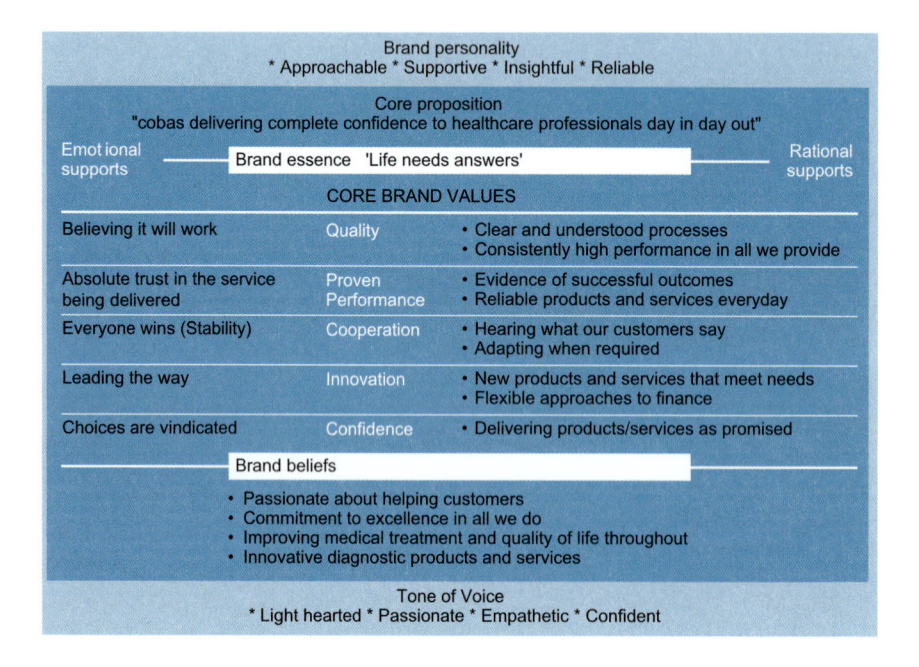

Figure 6.17 How Roche Diagnostics marketers turned customer values into brand values
Source: Roche Diagnostics

individual to have exactly the right treatment. The sub-brand therefore deliberately emphasizes the additional value Customized.

By developing cobas Cardio as a sub-brand, Roche Diagnostics could stretch its appeal beyond the relatively narrow field of a diagnostic equipment/testing brand to evolve towards a brand that is seen – by doctor and patient alike – as one that helps to address the condition as a whole. In this way, Roche could fine-tune the marketing of specific products/sub-brands. And in doing so, it could also influence diagnostic equipment sales, with patients and doctors specifying which diagnostic equipment and tests they want used.

Thus cobas – with the brand slogan 'Life needs answers' – emerged as a strategic brand initiative that helped Roche Diagnostics tackle all of its problems at the same time: to strengthen its position in the market (clear brand positioning, increased doctor/patient influence on purchasing decision), rationalize its brand portfolio, and drive marketing efficiencies (with a single global brand creating greater market impact for lower total cost).

These results were achieved *without* the use of tools such as archetypes, joint space mapping, or customer base analysis. In this case, these tools weren't appropriate. Tools such as these are designed to help the *application* of a values-based approach to strategic brand management. But values analysis can and does work without them.

PUTTING THINGS IN PERSPECTIVE

When push comes to shove, effective brand strategy boils down to two simple questions:

◆ **Brand portfolio and architecture:** how many brands do we need, to do what particular jobs?

◆ **Brand positioning:** how should these brands present themselves within the marketplace?

As every marketer knows, however, such apparently simple questions can create some very complicated answers, full of dilemmas and tensions. The case studies above illustrate some of these dilemmas, and show how a values-based approach to brand management helped chart a way forward. In the case of Esprit, values analysis helped identify new brand positionings. In the case of Accor, values analysis helped solve a knotty set of problems relating to the brand portfolio, including when and whether to drop brands, merge brands, or co-brand. This, in turn, helped marketers develop clear positionings. In the case of Roche, the values-based approach helped to solve both brand portfolio and brand positioning problems at the same time.

Of course, every brand situation is unique. The specifics of each challenge always differ, and so does the application of the necessary tools. Here are a few more examples of how values analysis can help strategy formulation.

Realizing the need for a new brand

A consumer products company was trying to extend its market (from primarily men to women). Because it was offering the new market basically the same products, it planned to extend its current brand. However, values analysis of the two groups of customers revealed that their values profiles were almost entirely opposite. The values adopted by men were rejected by women, and vice versa. Any 'umbrella' brand attempting to appeal to both groups would inevitably end up alienating one of them. Even though the company was selling basically the same products, it realized it needed to create a completely separate brand for its new audience.

Eliminating unnecessary sub-brands

Edeka, the leading German food retailer, had developed a range of store formats, each with its own sub-brand. But an analysis of shopper values – the actual value proposition of each format – showed no significant difference between them. Further research showed that consumers did not recognize the sub-brands: they saw themselves as shopping at Edeka. This gave Edeka the chance to scrap its complex brand strategy and focus all resources on building just one brand, Edeka itself.

Positioning the same brand in different markets

As part of a retrenchment process, Marks & Spencer (M&S), the iconic UK retailer, withdrew from many of its directly owned international activities. But it still had a number of franchised stores operating in countries such as Hungary, the Philippines, and Greece. M&S wanted to build a consistent brand identity across these international operations, but in a way that allowed franchisees considerable leeway in their local activities. It used the values profile to identify its actual value proposition – the values of the people who actually use the brand – across every franchised market. It then looked at the common features of all these brand profiles to identify common attributes. It used these common attributes to identify a common 'core' of the M&S brand internationally, while allowing franchisees to target additional values according to the needs of local markets.

Repositioning brands

A second problem faced by Edeka was that the values embraced by its customers did not give it the position it wanted in the marketplace. In order to differentiate itself in the market – especially from discounters – it needed to emphasize service and quality. So it developed a new 'target' value proposition to emphasis service, quality, and range. This became the basis for all subsequent marketing activities, including its first television advertising on such a strong 'branded' theme. Very specific guidelines were developed to ensure consistent execution of the new brand proposition.

Aligning business partners

Bunte, a German celebrity/gossip magazine, faced a problem with its advertisers. While its editorial was aimed at one consumer segment, advertisers saw it as targeting other segments. There was a clash between its glossy, glitzy editorial content and the style of the ads it carried. A profile revealing the values of its readers – compared with the profiles of advertisers it wanted to attract to the magazine – helped to create a better fit between editorial content and the advertising it carried. When advertisers saw the magazine's brand profile they could see how the magazine's readers fitted their brands.

THE DIRTY DOZEN REVISITED

Back in Chapter 1 we outlined brand management's 'dirty dozen.' We suggested that the dirty dozen had a common 'cause': that too many companies were starting their brand management strategies from the wrong place – a bit like Theseus deploying his Ariadne-thread from some starting place inside the labyrinth, when he was already lost. Then in Chapters 2, 3, and 4 we outlined a different philosophy and approach to brand management based on understanding customers' values, as well as product or service needs and requirements. In this chapter we explored how this different approach can bear fruit in richer, sharper strategy.

But has this alternative approach helped address the 'dirty dozen' pitfalls? Let's see.

1 Disconnect between strategy and tactics

Because people's values don't change quickly, a values-based approach to brand management focuses marketers' minds on long-term fundamentals, not short-term pressures. However, at the same time, the development of TVPs (target value propositions) gives marketers clear guidelines for implementation, based on the same data and same analysis.

2 Erratic processes

Ensuring consistency across the marketing mix will always be a significant operational challenge. However, TVPs provide a real Ariadne-thread to marketers struggling to keep their perspective during the day-to-day hurly-burly of marketing implementation, including managing agency relationships.

3 Limited customer insight

The trouble with most market research is that it does just that: it researches previously identified and clearly delineated 'markets' for products. Because the research focuses on the product – looking at users only in so far as their usage directly affects product attributes – within these preset parameters, most research results tend to converge on the same points. High levels of 'product parity' are a direct consequence of product-focused research. By looking at the values of people and how these values are made manifest within markets, marketers can gain a much clearer insight into what is driving different segments in which directions. Clearly focused, differentiated brands follow from such insights.

4 Lack of analytical rigor

The ability to quantify the relative economic attractiveness of different segments and strategies – in line with the brand attributes each such segment is looking for – has been demonstrated in this chapter. Values-based brand management is rigorous from start to finish.

5 Data incompatibility

Case studies in this chapter and the next show how, by making values the pivotal centre of gravity of all analysis, the values-based approach creates data integration instead of incompatibility.

6 No common language

Probably no company will ever be completely free of this disease. But by creating a fact-based and easily visualizable methodology which spans both hard financial data and 'soft' brand issues, the values-based approach helps minimize the problem.

7 Bureaucracy

The values approach forces managers to focus on the facts of the marketing case rather than simply follow 'business as usual' assumptions.

8 Silo-itis

Getting departments such as advertising and customer service to talk and work together is an endless challenge. But by creating a common framework and language, the values-based approach helps bring down the barriers.

9 Brand narcissism

Values-based brand management is a constant reminder to marketers that their brand is defined by the people who buy it, not by marketers' own visions. If there is no alignment with the target market, there is effectively no brand.

10 Confusing brand architectures

Values-based brand management creates a logical framework for defining brand portfolios and architectures. If the values of different groups of users are very different, a different brand or sub-brand is needed.

11 Poor innovation

By working from peoples' values back to the offering – and using tools such as joint space analysis – the values-based approach helps identify gaps in the market.

12 Fence sitting

Values-based brand management demonstrates the counter-productive nature of fence sitting and helps quantify the benefits of building truly distinctive brands.

SUMMARY

In this chapter we have reviewed how values-related data can be used to identify the most economically attractive customer segments; to analyze how effectively the brand is currently attracting these most attractive segments (customer base analysis); to analyze where the brand stands in relation to its main competitors (joint space analysis); and to turn these analyses into the formation of a target value proposition, and assess the relative merits of alternative TVPs (brand strategy scorecards).

We have seen how companies have used these tools and techniques to identify growth opportunities, reposition brands, clarify and rationalize brand portfolios, and build more coherent, logical brand architectures. Along the way, we have seen how this methodology – deploying the Ariadne-thread of values profiles – helps us avoid the 'dirty dozen' brand management pitfalls.

The starting point for the use of values in the brand management process is a company's history. Everything the organization has done in the past – its products, communications, and so on – has come together to create the current situation. The brand's 'actual value proposition' (AVP) is defined by the values of the people who choose to buy that brand. This AVP shows where, and by how much, the values of the brand's buyers differ from those of the population as a whole.

Although the brand management process is usually considered end-to-end, here a point needs to be stressed. The values-based approach can 'enter the equation' at any point: at the beginning in terms of analysis, in the middle of strategy formulation, or at the end of execution. Ideally, of course, it would inform the whole process. That way its Ariadne-thread benefits are maximized. But even if it is used to focus on just one part of the process, it can help.

Using marketers' accumulated understanding of the company and the market, and aided by tools such as customer base analysis and joint space mapping, a TVP can then be developed. This TVP identifies the values the brand intends to appeal to, and those it plans to distance itself from. The differences between the AVP and the TVP help reveal what needs to be done next. This involves everything the brand does: the product itself, its pricing strategy, marketing communications, and so on. Typically this involves emphasizing some existing values a little more, dropping some others, and adding some new ones. Clearly a road map needs to be devised for this: it may be dangerous to do it all at one time. Each step towards the TVP needs to be identified, and executed at the right time.

This raises a fundamental point: if the resulting strategy is not implemented well and consistently, all the previous work will have been a waste of time. Without excellent implementation, values-based brand strategies (indeed any brand strategies at all) are little more than useless. The difference is that with our values-based analysis behind us, we can use the same thinking and the same data to improve implementation too. The same Ariadne-thread helps us work our way through every practical detail of the brand's core offering, communication content, and communication strategy. That is the subject of Chapter 7.

7   From brand strategy to action

Values-based brand management

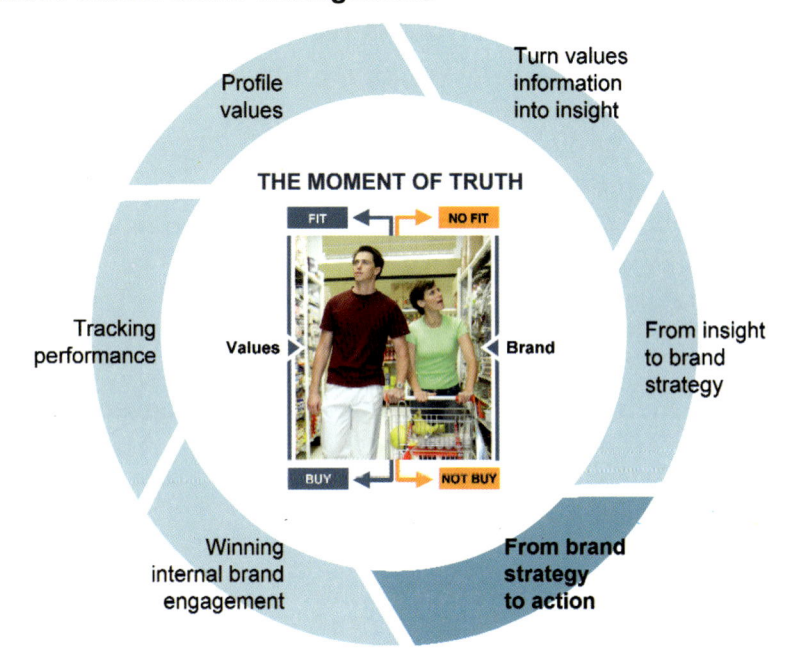

It goes without saying: even the most superb strategy is worthless unless it is implemented – and implemented well. Yet this is precisely where many companies' marketing efforts fall short.

Sometimes this is simply because operational excellence is so hard to achieve. Actually making things happen requires discipline, attention to detail, and motivation: the difference between mediocre and best in class is often huge. It is much easier to get the timing of the promotions materials out of sync with the ad campaign, to have the materials stuck at the back of the store rather than on display, than it is to get everything humming together in perfect synergy.

But often plans aren't executed well because of the fundamental disconnects we talked about earlier: between 'marketing' and the rest of the company; between brand strategy and corporate strategy; between general direction and detailed application. There isn't an Ariadne-thread clearly linking them.

This is often compounded by a divide between 'creative' marketing and agency types, and 'rational,' data-driven accountants and operational experts. Sometimes stressing the need for 'creativity' is just a smokescreen to hide flaky thinking and an inability (or unwillingness) to quantify options or measure results. But at root, marketing is a creative process; knowing how to engage people's attention, and connect with them, requires genuine creativity. The point is, creativity needs focus – and a values-based approach provides this, as well as the links between brand and corporate strategy.

The critical connection is provided by the target value proposition (TVP). Once we have identified the values the brand needs to address (and the values the brand wants to distance itself from), our understanding of these values can be used to:

◆ redefine the actual offer – products, services, features, and so on

◆ communicate in a clear, consistent coherent way, across all customer touch points and media channels.

In this way it is possible to create a seamless connection between strategy and execution, and 'product' and 'communication.'

Left as abstract phrases, values such as New and cool or 24/7 pro-tech are meaningless. They only connect with people – they only have meaning – when these values are embedded within and expressed by the products and services the company offers. Take Accor. Once it had

> It goes without saying that strategy is useless if it is not implemented – and implemented well. The device of the TVP creates a clear link between strategic targeting decisions and implementation. Knowing which values we are targeting helps define every element of the marketing mix.

understood the values of different groups of customers, it could tweak hotel decors and services to address them: cutting out fancy restaurants, but adding in state-of-the-art business support facilities for Performers, for example.

At Roche Diagnostics, also discussed in the last chapter, marketers were concerned that competitors were seen as being much more dynamic and innovative. The downside of being seen as 'a safe bet' – 'no one ever got fired for buying IBM' – is that the brand comes to be seen as being stodgy, behind the times, and not up to speed. Roche therefore needed to improve its reputation for innovation. But at the same time, its values research revealed the danger of going overboard. Among Roche's customers, values such as Proven and Quality were paramount. Roche needed to keep on stressing its strength in these areas – while adding a tinge of innovation at the edges. That's very different from positioning the brand as being at the forefront of innovation: innovation is important, but not at the risk of jettisoning the core values of Proven and Quality.

So how to bring values alive through products and services?

CASE STUDY: SPRINGFIELD

Springfield, a successful Spanish men's retailer, was less successful than planned with its move into the German market: it was failing to differentiate itself clearly enough. An analysis of its marketing performance highlighted two problems. First, it had not communicated its value proposition strongly and clearly enough: the brand was suffering from low awareness. Second, the value proposition itself was not clear enough.

Springfield's core target market was men between 18 and 40. Analyzing this group, rather than the population as a whole, revealed five distinct clusters or archetypes (see Figure 7.1).

The biggest group by far were what Springfield decided to call 'Hedonistic performers', with a strong focus on the values of 24/7 pro-tech, Personal efficiency, and Customized. They accounted for 43 percent of the total market and 49 percent of its value. Further analysis of Springfield's customer base showed this group to be particularly important to Springfield. A specific sub-group of Hedonistic performers – dubbed 'high performers' – were ten times more likely to be heavy spenders at

German men aged 18-40 years

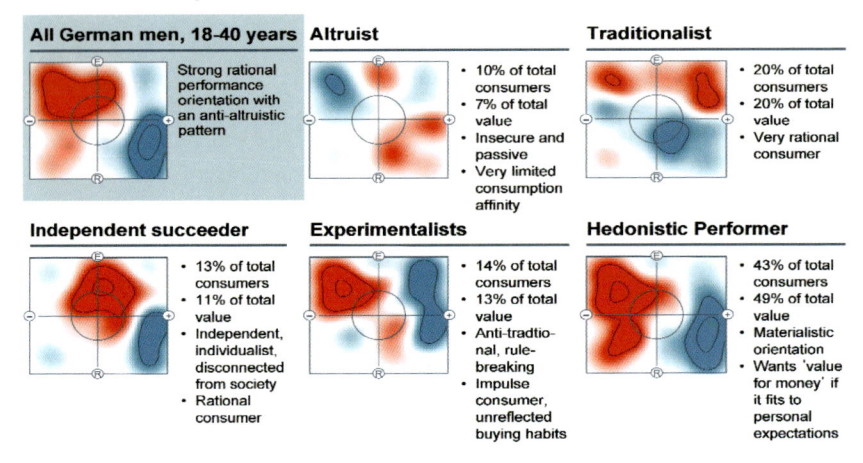

Figure 7.1 How the values of male clothes buyers differ (Germany)
Source: Roland Berger Strategy Consultants, Roland Berger Market Research data (Germany, October/November 2002, n=1532, population 12–65 years, CATI)

Springfield stores than German men as a whole. In addition, even though Springfield's brand was weak (the values of its users were not that different from the population as a whole), those leanings that could be identified were towards the hedonistic performer segment.

Springfield therefore developed a new TVP focusing strongly on the core values of 24/7 pro-tech, Personal efficiency, and backed by a lighter emphasis on Customized and New and cool, plus Quality and Service (which had been markedly absent from its current user base). Figure 7.2 shows how the new TVP maps against the values of its current users. The TVP does not contradict the values of current users; it emphasizes these values much more strongly, while trying to build up new strengths such as Quality and Service.

Figure 7.2 also shows how, by visualizing the TVP in this way, competitor strengths and weaknesses can be taken into account. The new emphasis on Quality and Service would, for example, help Springfield differentiate itself from Zara and Hennes & Mauritz, while a greater emphasis on New and cool would help attract borderline customers from them.

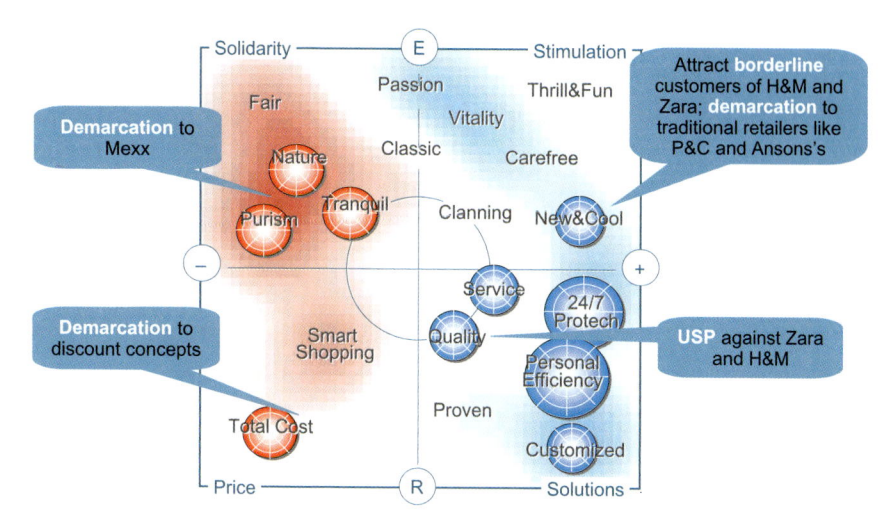

Figure 7.2 Springfield's new TVP mapped against the values of its current users
Source: Roland Berger Strategy Consultants

Likewise by embracing some strong anti-values too, Springfield could differentiate itself against other competitors such as Mexx on the one hand and discounters on the other.

Springfield buyers, marketers, and merchandisers could now focus on a new, very clear target segment: the high performer. And thanks to their previous values-based research they had a very good idea of what this person looked like.

He was twice as likely to be over 26 as under, and his monthly income was in the region of €2500, with around €1000 spent on clothes every year, 28 percent of it (currently) at Springfield. He was probably employed full time (75 percent had full-time jobs, 25 percent were students), and preferred a relatively formal and classic-oriented fashion style for business, with half this group regularly wearing a suit or shirt and pants. When shopping, he tended to be destination-driven, looking for one-stop solutions. And he had high brand loyalty. In terms of attitudes and values, he was progressive, assertive, and competitive, with a strong focus on performance. He was not particularly price sensitive, but did have a value-for-money orientation. His approach was rational and slightly traditional, though he was interested in new trends.

The challenge for Springfield was then to apply this broad positioning to its store portfolio (where its stores were located), to everything it did in store, and to its communications. To do this it needed to review everything through the eyes of core values: how does this or that detail embed, encapsulate, and express a value like 24/7 pro-tech or Personal efficiency?

Thus, for example, a twin approach to store locations was developed: flagship city-center stores, backed by supporting outlets in middle-class consumer environments and near to protagonist areas (the contrast between Schadowstrasse and Flinger Strasse in Düsseldorf, or Kaufinger Strasse and Hohenzollernstrasse in Munich). The stores themselves needed to look different. Among the necessary changes were to reduce wooden elements and increase chrome/glass fixtures, stone floors, and spotlights to come across as more modern and rational; to make stores spotlessly clean and efficient to use (with minimal queues for dressing rooms); and to use state-of-the-art technology in store (such as television screens, cash registers, and fitting rooms). Even the cash register sends a values message.

Both the product range and its visual merchandising needed to change too. Springfield needed to increase its focus on straight smart casual outfits and to expand its formal wear. It also needed to create clearly identified solution or competence areas focusing on different usage occasions. Merchandising approaches needed to appeal to rational performer types: clear and tidy, aiding decisions at a glance, with easy-to-find items. (Full-color blocking of merchandise may look good, but it appeals to a different set of values.) Likewise, store windows needed to be clear and simple, not overcrowded.

Springfield marketers also had to remember the values in the round: not each value in isolation, but their combination. Getting the right balance is crucial. Thus, even though the brand's main focus was on 24/7 pro-tech and Personal efficiency, it also wanted to emphasize the more emotional value of New and cool. One way to do so was to create special stimulation areas focused (for example) on sports themes or co-marketing events.

Service needed to change too. A customized orientation makes helpful fitting room staff a must (helping with sizing, styling tips, and so on). Over-loud music was to be avoided, in favor of a more middle-of-the-road approach. Staff were to be recruited to act as fashion role models.

Finally, communications strategies also needed to adapt. An analysis of the projected value proposition – the values actually expressed in ad campaigns and other communications materials – showed that the brand had previously appealed more to a different archetype (Experimentalists) than to the Hedonistic performers now identified as its core market. 'Rule-breaking' had been a major theme in former advertising, but rule-breaking was not a major attraction for those more concerned with service, quality, technology, and customization. (We return to communications and intended and projected value propositions in more detail below.)

Store locations, store design and ambience, merchandising, staffing, service, and communication: all of these factors were addressed by Springfield's new TVP – and thanks to the clarity of this proposition, they could be addressed consistently in a synergistic way. Everybody could understand what the company was trying to do and why. The logic and connections were clear for all to see. Strategy could be turned into detailed actions.

CASE STUDY: CHEMICALS COMPANY (GERMANY)

Ah, but!, you might say. Of course it is a good idea to apply a values-based approach to branding to a strongly values-focused industry such as fashion. But what about much more rational markets such as, say, commodity chemicals? Surely the same approach won't work there? Well, it appears that it can.

A major chemicals supplier analyzed its customer base according to the values of its customers. Along the way it discovered something that has been said many times before but is forgotten just as often: a commodity is more of a mindset than a market state. If you look at the product in isolation, a commodity mindset is almost impossible to avoid. But if you look at why different customers buy the product and how they use it, significant differences – and therefore opportunities for differentiation – usually emerge.

Analyzing customer motives and processes actually brought six very different segments to light. They were:

♦ Image buyers, who trusted the famous-name brand of the supplier instead of rationally comparing product and price attributes with other suppliers.

♦ Quality buyers, who purchased goods from this supplier because of its consistent adherence to quality specifications such as ingredient purity.

♦ Price buyers, who saw all players as offering the same basic quality and service, leaving price as the deciding factor.

♦ Convenience buyers, who were most interested in easy transactions and streamlined processes.

♦ Relationship buyers, who looked for intensive and often personal support from the supplier in terms of expertise, advice and so on.

♦ Process partners, for whom reliable and transparent logistics services, along with stable pricing, were key.

Each of these different groups generated different margin contributions for the firm. While price buyers were the biggest segment (with the lowest margin contributions), they still accounted for less than 25 percent of all sales. The smallest segment – quality buyers – delivered the highest margins. Together, the two most profitable segments accounted for 30 percent of total sales.

The supplier then recalibrated its value proposition segment by segment. For price buyers, it stopped offering add-on technology applications and started charging extra for small orders, special logistics arrangements, and so on. It addressed the priorities of quality and relationship buyers by sending its experts on visits to their plants to provide advice on the best use of its products. For process partners on the other hand, it introduced vendor-managed inventory services.

It also initiated actions to move customers from one segment to another: explaining to price buyers the reputational risks of buying lower-quality products, for example. A thorough analysis of each segment and the likely effects of these initiatives suggested a 15 percent improvement in profitability in this so-called commodity segment was possible. In fact, when the changes were implemented the profit improvement was even higher. Happier customers proved willing to pay a higher price or to become less demanding in price negotiations.

The final, often clinching, piece of marketing implementation is communication: what the brand says, and how it delivers this message, in terms of both chosen channel and budget. Values-based strategies can help on both fronts. Let's look at message content first.

CASE STUDY: YORN

Yorn is a youth-oriented mobile phone brand launched by Telecel in Portugal in 2000. At the time, Yorn's TVP was clear: the brand would address the values of New and cool, 24/7 pro-tech, Clanning, and Passion – with a clear distance between itself and values such as Classic, Tranquil, and Proven (see Figure 7.3). These were earmarked as being 'off limits' for the brand. Instead, they were merely left as a trap for the competition.

Early ad campaigns were faithful to this brand strategy, but after a while the creative execution began to drift. The brand began to lose momentum and a review of its projected value proposition showed why.

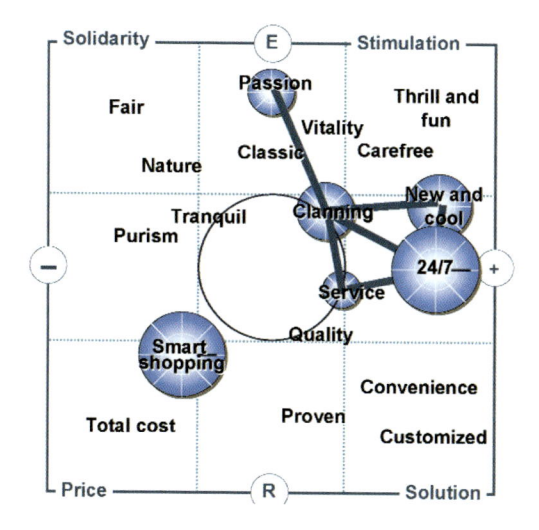

Figure 7.3 Yorn's original target value proposition
Source: Roland Berger Strategy Consultants

Figure 7.4 shows the *projected* value proposition of the Yorn brand over time. To analyze a projected value proposition, a panel of internal and external experts assesses the values content of the brand's communications and compares the values projected to audiences with the brand's TVP. This can be a painstaking process. It needs to be done ad by ad, promotion by promotion, direct mail shot by direct mail shot. Advertisements may need to be analyzed execution by execution and if necessary frame by frame.

In the case of Yorn, the results of such a projected value proposition analysis were daunting.

Figure 7.4 shows the values analysis of four Yorn television campaigns over time. The indicators give an assessment of how close to the TVP the actual communication was. Moving from top left to bottom right:

◆ The *first campaign* expressed the value New and cool very clearly (as intended). Other values also made a showing, largely as intended: Clanning, Carefree, Passion.

◆ The *second campaign* 'forgot' all these original values to focus on Thrill and fun and Smart shopping, with a strong anti-Tranquil message.

◆ The *third campaign* was almost entirely negative: strongly anti-Fair, anti-Clanning (one of the original positive values), and anti-Proven.

◆ The *fourth campaign* placed its strongest pro-emphasis on Smart shopping, with an equally strong rejection of Fair.

Not only did the campaigns not keep to the brand's TVP, they were also inconsistent with each other. They wandered all over the place in a self-contradictory way. No wonder Yorn's prospective customer base was confused!

Meanwhile, as the brand's market performance faltered, other marketing mechanics took higher priority. The Yorn brand appeared on all manner of sponsorships, apparently willy-nilly. Promotions and ads borrowed themes and ideas from mainstream marketing trends and media blockbusters – thereby undermining the message of New and cool. A succession of price promotions and give-aways made the brand seem cheap.

Projected value propositions

Selected advertising campaigns

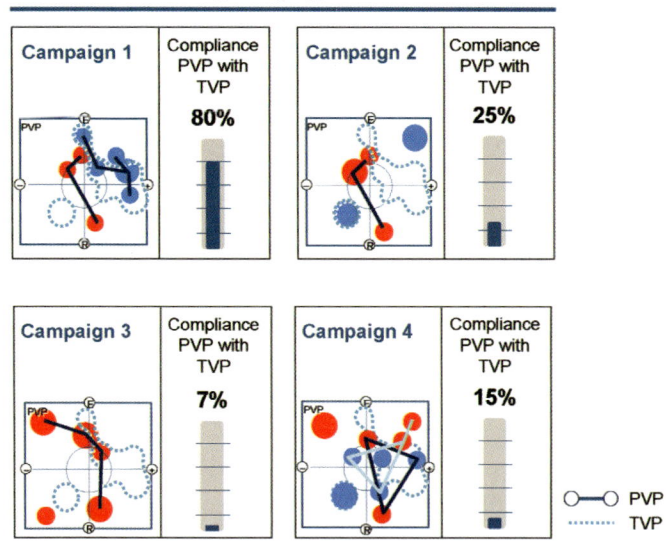

Figure 7.4 Comparing the values Yorn communicated with what it originally intended
Source: Roland Berger Strategy Consultants

Without the 'backbone' of the brand's core TVP, its communications had lost all sense of direction. After a couple of years of increasingly desperate, and disparate, marketing activities, the brand was in a mess (see Figure 7.5). A profile of the users of the brand showed them to be anti many things but pro hardly anything. The brand was no longer addressing any positive market drivers: its original positive focus values like New and cool and 24/7 pro-tech had gone out of the window.

Luckily for Yorn marketers, the fact that they could track the progress of their marketing activities against the TVP – and test out how well each execution of the marketing strategy helped or hindered this process – allowed them to identify the problem early enough to get back on track.

Once they had identified the problem, all that was needed was for every television commercial, promotion, and sponsorship exercise to reinforce these same basic values – in new and fresh ways.

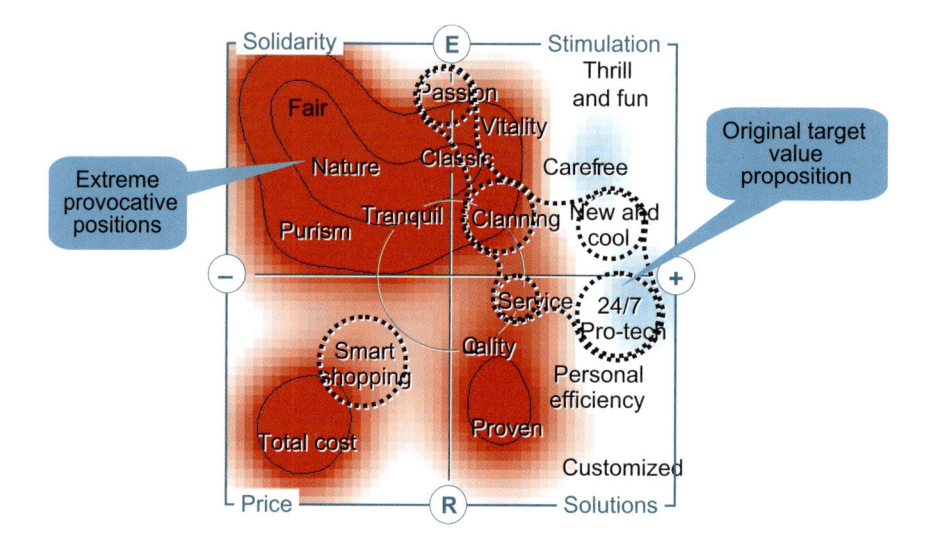

Figure 7.5 Yorn's actual value proposition before its repositioning
Source: Roland Berger Strategy Consultants

CASE STUDY: CONSUMER PRODUCTS COMPANY (HUNGARY)

But even the right creativity gets wasted without the right media and channel strategy. This is the final loop of the Ariadne-thread offered by values-based strategy. Figure 7.6 shows a disguised example of how it can work. The company concerned is a world market leader in a male-oriented consumer product – let's call it Alpha – and wanted to extend its market to women. Marketing logic, traditional brand logic, and production logic all seemed to suggest a straightforward brand extension: 'Alpha for women.' But a profile of female users' values revealed them to be very different from male users (see Figure 5.3, page 70). Any brand attributes or product features designed to attract men were likely to put off women, and vice versa. A new brand (endorsed by the parent company in a low-key way) was needed.

The next question was how to present this brand to the new target market. Previous values-based analysis had identified the most economically attractive consumer segments, what the product needed to offer to attract them, and what the communications

Managing agencies

Time and time again, the best-laid marketing plans are diverted and ruined by brand managers' inability to manage their advertising and other agencies.

A brief is sent to the agency. The agency's 'creatives' get to work and a new ad campaign is brought back to the client for approval. On what basis should the work be judged? Whether we 'like it' or not? How creative it seems? How well it pre-tests for getting the message through? In which case, is it absolutely clear what the message actually is?

In Yorn's case, the agency kept to the brief in its first campaign but by the second campaign, the agency's creatives had shaken off the discipline of the brand's TVP and were busy doing their own thing. Campaigns that followed were all very creative – but they had nothing to do with the brand's target market or message.

By analyzing each piece of creative work against whether or not it addresses the values identified by the TVP, each piece of agency work can be assessed against a clear, demonstrable test: does the projected value proposition address our target values or not?

This tool is especially helpful for non-marketing experts (such as the board) to decide whether or not to go ahead with a particular campaign – or agency.

needed to emphasize. Returning to the same data bank allowed the company's marketers to make the connections between this target customer segment and their shopping and media consumption habits: not only what to reach them with, but how best to reach them. It was therefore possible for marketers to say, 'If we want to attract these types of people, we know they tend to shop at these stores, watch these television programs, read these magazines, and so on.'

For this target audience, for example, two key retailers stood out: Tesco and the Co-Op. And classic prime-time television advertising

Consumer product, Hungary

Focus	• Female Hungarians in the age group 14–25		
Age segment(s)	• First timers in the age group 14–19 • Young women segment (age 20–29)	TV channel [1]	• RTL Klub: 100.0% • Viva: 71.4% • TV2: 56.6%
Status	• Non brand users	Time of TV watching	• After 6pm: 72.7% • 3pm–6pm: 28.5%
Product group	• [defined products]	Radio station [1]	• Danubius: 69.1% • Other: 65.4% • Juventus, Rádiól: 34.6%
Usage intensity	• Weekly: 70.6% • Monthly: 29.4%	Time of radio listening	• After 6pm: 69.1%
Shopping location [1]	• Tesco: 25.9% • Other places: 25.7% • Coop: 24.9%	Print media [1]	• Story: 43.9% • Meglepetés: 43.3% • Bravo Girl: 42.5%
Shopping frequency	• Monthly: 50.6% • Every 3 months: 49.4%	Consumption level [3]	• 500–1,000 HUF: 25.7% • Less than 500 HUF: 24.9% • 1,000–2,000 HUF: 23.6%

1) Multiple response   2) Based on n=1, Nr. 4: DM, Rossmann: 23,6%   3) Claimed yearly category consumption

Figure 7.6 Connecting consumer segments to retail and media channel choices (disguised)
Source: Roland Berger Strategy Consultants, TNS data (Hungary, September 2004, n=2011, population 14–70 years, CATI)

on two Hungarian stations (RTL Klub and Viva) emerged as the most efficient communication opportunity.

Similar analyses for different product groups identified different retailers and different media. For existing male users, for example, MTV emerged as a key television channel, and so did Danubius radio, and print media in the form of Blikk, Nemzeti Sport, and Népszabadság (Figure 7.7). Thus values data not only helped to identify the target market and shape product and communications development, it also helped to precisely target trade promotions and media advertising. Auchan emerged as a key distribution point too.

Such analyses can also have a major influence on the size of marketing budgets. Once the values and behaviors of the target audience are understood, the best way to reach them also becomes easier to identify. In some cases brands need to raise their profile and spend more on advertising (or at least spend differently). But in other cases, cost savings simply 'drop out' of the analysis. Thus for example,

Consumer product, Hungary

Focus	• Current male brand users		
Age segment(s)	• All age segments	TV channel [1]	• RTL Klub: 81.5% • TV2: 71.2% • MTV: 50.7%
Status	• Users of brand (all product types) and users of rival brands	Time of TV watching	• After 6pm: 89.4% • 3pm–6pm: 17.2% • 9am–3pm: 8.8%
Product group	• Male oriented products	Radio station [1]	• Danubius: 43.7% • Sláger rádió: 41.1% • Kossuth: 28.0%
Usage intensity	• 3 times a week: 26.1% • 2 times a week: 17.9% • 4 times a week: 15.1%	Time of radio listening	• 9am–3pm: 45.7% • 6am–9am: 45.6% • 3pm–6pm: 35.0%
Shopping location [1]	• Tesco: 35.9% • Small private place: 24.3% • Auchan: 20.5%	Print media [1]	• Blikk: 26.4% • Nemzeti Sport: 12.7% • Népszabadság: 11.1%
Shopping frequency	• Monthly: 51.2% • Every 3 months: 32.2% • Every 6 months: 8.3%	Consumption level [2]	• 1,000–2,000 HUF: 32.8% • 500–1,000 HUF: 23.6% • 2,000–3,000 HUF: 20.5%

1) Multiple response   2) Claimed yearly category consumption

Figure 7.7 Connecting consumers to retail and media channels (disguised)
Source: Roland Berger Strategy Consultants, TNS data (Hungary, September 2004, n=2011, population 14–70 years, CATI)

Esprit was concerned that it was spending large amounts of money on image advertising and seeing limited sales uplifts in return. Analyzing the values of the target market showed why: they are far more influenced by their peer groups, word of mouth, and editorial. The new marketing communications strategy therefore took a different tack: tie-ups with television programs popular with the target audience (such as MTV and various soap operas); PR in magazines targeting the same group; music sponsorship; organizing online talent contests; plus a much greater emphasis on in-store theater and design. The net effect was much greater communications effectiveness – at a much lower total cost.

Roche Diagnostics was also able to achieve greater communications effectiveness at lower total cost, this time by rationalizing its brand portfolio. Over the years, across its various business areas, Roche Diagnostics' brands had multiplied and lost any real sense of coherence (see Figure 7.8). Every time a new product came to market, a new brand name was invented, creating clutter and confusion for

BEFORE | AFTER

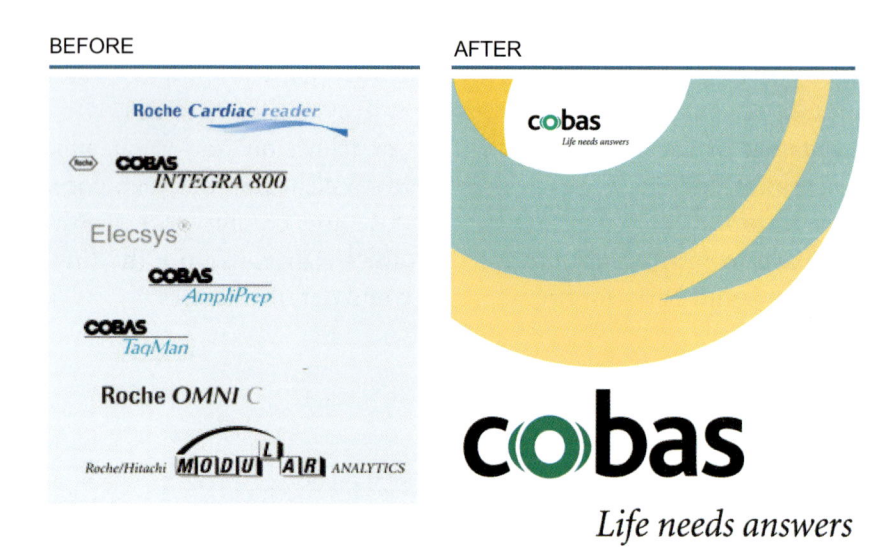

Figure 7.8 How Roche Diagnostics rationalized its brand portfolio to create critical mass
Source: Roche Diagnostics

both Roche and its customers. By shifting to one single umbrella brand – with a much more emotional appeal – Roche Diagnostics was able to create clarity, simplicity, stand out from the competition, and reach critical mass in terms of marketing communications investment. This would not have been possible if the underlying values analysis had not identified common values among all the key Roche Diagnostics customers (see Chapter 6 case study, page 107).

SUMMARY

Experience shows that frequent disconnects between marketers and their corporate peers, between product and communication, and between tactics and strategy, reflect a deeper problem: that most brand strategies start in the wrong place, and it is this wrong starting place that creates the disconnects.

We need the marketing equivalent of an Ariadne-thread to hold all these activities, perspectives, and people together, and guide us through the marketing maze. A values-based approach to brand strategy provides us with such an Ariadne-thread. It takes us all the way from initial research and analysis, through insight generation and strategy formulation, to the precise details of implementation – right down to the content of the ad, on which radio or television station, at which time. And it does so in a way that creates a clear link between corporate and brand strategy, between product and communication (they both have to reflect and address the values that constitute the brand backbone), and between broad strategy and detailed tactics.

Ariadne's thread at work

Values-based brand management provides the hard data and the insight to both formulate and implement brand strategies, from the creation of a TVP to fine-tuning the marketing mix, down to the finest details of media buying, and the analysis and approval of marketing communications activities.

We also noted the familiar debate about creativity, and the difficulty 'creative' types have in seeing eye to eye with data-driven, highly 'rational' managers in other departments. We accepted that, once the right strategy has been identified, creativity is often a decisive contributor to ultimate success. But, we added, by clearly defining the values we are addressing, a values-based approach to brand building provides a springboard for this creativity: it takes real, and ongoing, imagination and insight to turn a value such as New and cool, or Fair, or Customized, into a differentiated product or service proposition or a compelling advertising execution. Far from stifling the creative marketer's style and potential, a values-based approach to branding can be used to feed it. Marketing and agency creatives are no longer loose cannons. (We saw in the Yorn case study how damaging that can be.) They now understand exactly in which direction to shoot.

What's more, the board now has a clear framework to assess the essential creative sides of marketing. It may take a genius to come up with the creative idea that drives a marketing communications campaign in the first place. But as we saw with Yorn, any experienced executive can see whether it is addressing the value the brand wants to address – or whether it is veering off on a tangent.

When you're in a labyrinth it is easy to get lost. Without an Ariadne-thread to guide you, the chances of wandering down a blind alley multiply with each twist and turn. But an Ariadne-thread that gets broken is effectively useless. It's only when the link between research, analysis, strategy formulation, and final implementation is kept that its real potential is realized and we can emerge from the maze to enjoy the daylight.

Finally, we noted the need for detailed, dedicated implementation work. Execution is always crucial. The ability to execute well often marks the difference between winners and losers. With a product portfolio numbering tens of thousands, and operations in 150 countries, for example, Roche's adoption of its new diagnostics global brand cobas® has created a work agenda that requires disciplined, dedicated implementation for years ahead. The name, artwork, and marketing materials (look and feel) of literally thousands of stock-keeping units need to be changed, and staff and customers alike need to be informed about the logic and value of these changes. At the beginning of the changeover, Roche marketers estimated that it would take nearly a year simply to make sure Roche's own staff got the new picture; just the first phase of the implementation process would take at least three years, following a clear 'pecking order' of countries.

The success of the entire project depends on how well these detailed tasks are performed. And that in turn depends on whether the staff involved understand what they are supposed to be doing, and are fully motivated to do it. This is the final – and often the biggest – challenge of all brand strategies: the internal one.

8 Winning internal brand engagement

Values-based brand management

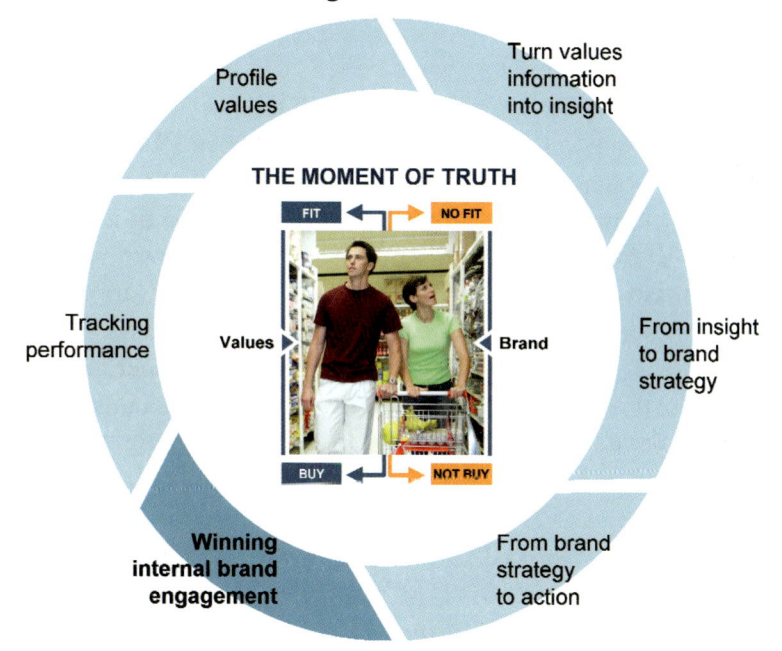

When brands were first invented they were simple selling propositions: messages sent from sellers to buyers. Branding was the way products were packaged and communicated. It was an 'inside-out' process – a way for the company to present its wares to external audiences. Branding and externally focused marketing communications were almost synonymous.

Over the years, however, branding has evolved. When retailers, telcos, financial services firms, and utilities embraced marketing and branding for example, they soon realized that advertising and packaging are often among the least important influences on overall customer perceptions. Other touch points – such as the experience of dealing with the company on the phone or face-to-face in a company outlet – are often a much greater influence. 'Touch point analysis' moved center stage, along with the need to coordinate and orchestrate the messages delivered by every touch point, whether it's a phone call, a bill, a face-to-face encounter with a member of staff, an advertisement or a promotional item. Ideally, companies realized, staff should act as 'brand ambassadors,' living the brand's values and meeting the brand's promises in front of customers' eyes. Branding was no longer just a 'mask' that was presented to outsiders. Staff behaviors and attitudes had entered the brand equation.

But the evolution hasn't stopped there. The more companies try to align their internal staff training and motivation programs with their external brand promise, the more 'brand engagement' works its way into the internal workings, culture, priorities, and even structures of the organization. 'Living the brand' isn't just for customer-facing staff, it applies to everyone because everyone is involved in delivering the brand's promise. (If they're not, then what value are they adding?) This in turn raises deep questions about the relationship between strategy, culture, and brand. How can we ask an employee to 'live the brand' if the brand's values do not align with, or express, the company's underlying culture and values? If there is a disconnect or contradiction it will be plainly obvious for everyone to see – and such disconnects are dangerous. They breed cynicism. They demotivate. They undermine rather than build brands.

The plus side is the huge internal potential of a strong brand. If the brand's promise and values are clear, inspiring – and demonstrably genuine – then the brand becomes a recruitment and management tool in its own right. Companies with successful brands find it much easier to recruit the best staff. They also find it much easier to motivate staff. And there's more. In companies where the brand really has taken root internally, the brand's values become a guide to day-to-day actions and priorities; embedded into targets, measures, reward systems, and career paths.

If a company is a 'low-cost producer,' then there are some things it always does and other things it never does. If it aims to be at the cutting edge of technical innovation or fashion, or renowned for world-class service, then some attitudes and behaviors become highly desirable and others highly undesirable.

We are back to our Ariadne-thread. For values-based strategic brand management to work, the values of customers outside the company need to connect with the values of the people who work inside the company.

Some companies have found these challenges easier than others. Companies such as Aldi, Ikea, Red Bull, Starbucks, and Virgin are famous for their strong internal cultures, and their brands have evolved more or less as a by-product of these cultures. Everyone, both inside and outside, 'knows' what the brand stands for. The same is true of fashion-oriented companies such as Nike.

But not all companies have it so easy. Sometimes markets change, and 'rebranding' becomes a necessity, as Roche Diagnostics discovered. Many companies have been involved in takeovers and mergers, and suddenly staff find themselves expected to switch brand loyalties (and associated attitudes and behaviors) almost overnight. A few years ago, for example, the UK-based oil giant BP purchased the German oil company Aral – a proud company with its own 100-year history. Is that history to suddenly mean nothing?

CASE STUDY: ROCHE DIAGNOSTICS

We saw in Chapter 6 how Roche Diagnostics used values-based analysis to better understand its different markets and recast its brand strategy. The resulting decision – a single brand called cobas® to cover all products from across four different business areas – left the company with a massive implementation challenge. Early estimates suggested that up to 32,000 different product lines would need to be renamed and repackaged. Thirteen thousand personnel from each business area, in 150 operating countries, all had to be involved. For senior management, the decision was easy: 'We have decided to do it, now do it!' In a highly decentralized company, actual detailed implementation would be a significant challenge.

Those responsible for implementation faced many potential hurdles. For a start, renaming and repackaging product lines required internal funding discussions: it's never an easy thing to win arguments about spending priorities. Every relevant communication had to be translated into local languages – and checked to make sure the meaning hadn't changed in the process.

And people's sensitivities had to be addressed. Roche had grown to be a very successful company on the back of technically oriented people producing products with names that they thought were brands. Many of these people had worked on these products for decades, and many didn't see branding as being a top priority anyway. Observes Harald F. Stock, senior vice president of Roche Diagnostic's Global Commercial Near Patient Testing Unit and sponsor of the project, 'People thought they had been doing the right thing, and they had been doing this for a long time. Now they had to accept the need to do something else. This was a big challenge.'

But the change went deeper still. Previously, when every product was effectively its own brand, a problem with one product wasn't contagious. If there was damage, it was effectively limited to that product. Now, with one umbrella brand covering a multitude of different products in different business areas, the reputational risks of making a mistake were much, much greater.

Meanwhile, marketers had to rethink the way they communicated with customers. Previously, communications had focused on technical

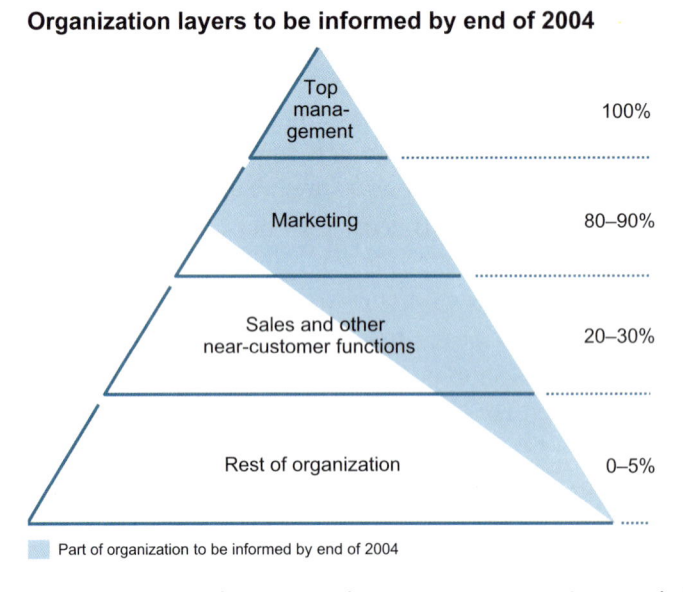

Organization layers to be informed by end of 2004

- Top management — 100%
- Marketing — 80–90%
- Sales and other near-customer functions — 20–30%
- Rest of organization — 0–5%

Part of organization to be informed by end of 2004

Figure 8.1 Roche's plan for getting the message across – in an orderly fashion
Source: Roland Berger Strategy Consultants

product features. Now marketers had to focus not only on the benefits these features delivered, but the values they embodied: values such as Quality, Proven, and Cooperation (the value identified as Clanning in the original consumer-focused methodology). This was a much more emotional approach to communication and it required the reworking of all marketing literature.

But the need to change was not confined to communications. Every function, including marketing, sales, production, and R&D, was faced with the need to re-examine its processes to make sure it was doing its best to bring the brand's values alive through everything it did. Instead of just focusing on technical performance, for example, researchers and developers needed to assess their work through the lens of the brand's values. How does what we are doing enhance (or perhaps threaten) our reputation for Proven, or Quality? 'Internally, it's about change management,' comments Stock.

So how has Roche addressed this challenge? The first thing it did was identify and appoint internal cobas 'brand ambassadors' for each country, making them the key contact points for the global roll-out and responsible for leading the implementation process in their country.

Different 'levels' of presentation were then developed, ranging from brief 'teaser' materials to alert employees to the fact that change was taking place, to in-depth explanations of the methodology used, the rationale for the changes, and the expected benefits and challenges – plus training toolkits to help pass on the message. Presentations were also adapted to the communication channel: from small in-depth training seminars to large 'town hall' staff meetings. 'Lots of talking' then followed, including briefings to and by senior managers, workshops targeted to different groups of specialists, and intensive three-day training sessions for those at the front line of implementation.

The sheer scale of the challenge also meant prioritization was necessary. Some target groups, and some key countries, were addressed first, followed by a planned roll-out across the company. First on the list were senior management and marketing, internationally. Then sales. Then the rest of the organization would follow later. All in all, the roll-out process would take at least two years. It's a massive task requiring disciplined, dedicated work: getting the troops on board internally is still very much a work in progress.

CASE STUDY: BP/ARAL

The challenging nature of internal brand engagement is underlined by our second case study: the BP/Aral merger in Germany. In July 2001 BP purchased the German oil company Aral from Eon, which immediately raised a strategic brand dilemma – should Aral petrol stations and products be rebranded as BP?

Ideally, for the sake of neatness and the development of BP as a global brand, the blue Aral brand, should have been replaced by the green of BP. But Aral was a famous, powerful brand in Germany with strong connotations for quality and cleanliness. BP, on the other hand, was not that well known in Germany. After intensive stakeholder research and much internal discussion, it was decided to keep Aral as the consumer-facing brand, with the added 'soft endorsement' of the BP logo in retail outlets and communications materials to convey the message that Aral is part of the BP stable.

Besides a review and analysis of external touch points for different external target groups, internal touch points and brand communication towards the organization's own employees also had to be analyzed, revised, and designed for the new BP look and feel. This, however, compounded the already formidable internal communications challenge created by the merger. The scale of the rebranding process was already huge: Aral's more than 4000 employees had to be brought into the BP fold. They were now BP employees and needed to think and act like BP employees. They had to absorb the corporate BP brand values Green, Innovative, Progressive, and Performance.

Yet while they were being told to have the green of the BP brand and its values in their hearts, their public face was still the blue of Aral. Bernd Vangerow, the project leader on the task, now global brand manager for BP, remembers that as long as the blue logos of Aral were still seen at every Germany petrol station, it was quite natural for employees to think, 'We are different because we stayed blue.' Indeed, looking back, Vangerow's own affinities were split. 'I had two hearts. One was green. The other was blue.' An additional hurdle in retaining a clear brand identity internally was the different language and culture.

So how can such challenges be confronted? By a combination of firmness, clarity, good planning, determination, humanity, and good old selling.

Firmness was needed to create symbolic acts that brought the change home to every employee. One example: requiring all staff to hand back their old (blue) Aral company identity cards to have them replaced with the new green of BP. To an important degree, these company cards express the identity of an employee. Changing the company cards was a signal that real identity change was under way.

Clarity and planning were needed for the main communications task. Analyzed employee touch points ranged across all business and service units. Every one of these touch points would now have to be retouched with green rather than blue – and every segment would need to hear the BP message in a way that spoke to the individuals and their situation via a media channel they used. Thus every possible channel of communication, from mugs and computer touchpads through internal magazines and newsletters, meetings, email, and the intranet was addressed in a planned way. So were the messages about BP's history, its strategy and plans, and its values.

Figure 8.2 illustrates the range and subtlety of the issues and audiences that needed to be encompassed by the messages and the discussions they generated.

But messaging alone is not enough. As the old saying goes, you can take a horse to water but you can't make it drink. More was needed to persuade employees to 'drink.' A key positive factor was the employee benefits of the merger – not general, remote benefits such as market share, but benefits that affected employees directly. There is a certain pride to be had from working for a highly visible, influential global company. Some employees were particularly motivated by BP's overall commitment to environmental issues. Others were excited by the global career opportunities that were now opening up: such opportunities simply didn't exist before.

Also, the human touch was needed. Social and cultural differences can't be addressed by brochures, notes Vangerow. They have to be addressed in person. So 'BP Living Rooms' were organized in every major facility. Each Living Room held a display of BP's history, current projects, values, and so on. Over a period of a year a whole series of informal events, meetings, and lunches were organized in the room, just to make sure that people met each other and started to understand one another. Top management played an important role, acting like role models and transferring BP brand values.

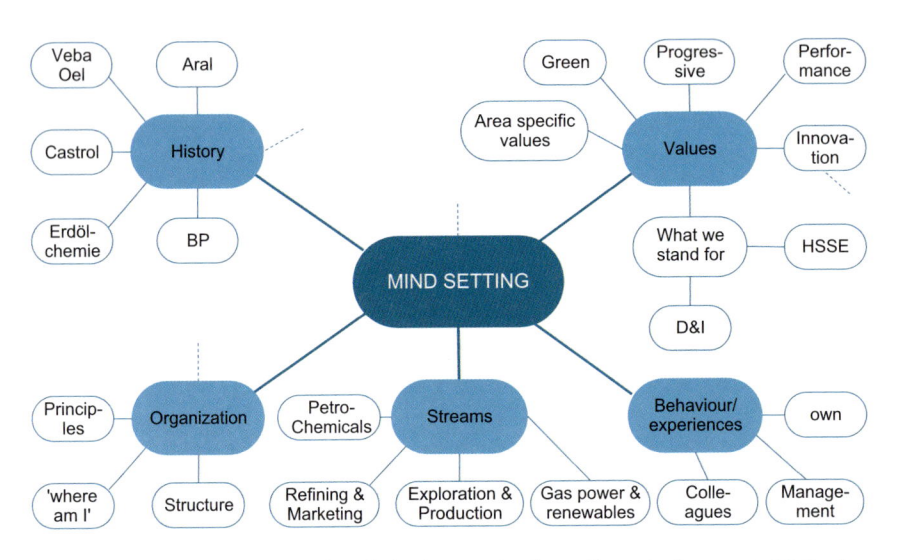

Figure 8.2 Assessing the scale of the internal rebranding challenge at BP/Aral
Source: BP, Project team 'Mind setting'

The learnings from BP/Aral are very similar to those of Roche. Internal brand engagement cannot be achieved by one-off campaigns. Nearly three years later the issues are still being addressed, notes Vangerow. 'This is work in progress. In a sense, getting employees to live the brand is a never-ending journey.' Ultimately, he suggests, for internal branding to really work, 'It is very important you have the right organizational structure.' Brand management needs to be a board position.

SUMMARY

It is sad but true: all the research suggests that in most companies most employees tend to be apathetic or disengaged rather than engaged in what the company is trying to do. Creating brand engagement and positive 'brand ambassadors' in such circumstances is very difficult. As both case studies emphasize, this whole area is still very much work in progress.

However, some learnings are already becoming apparent (see Figure 8.3). The general conclusion is that deliberately or by default, too many companies are still run on command-and-control lines where managers simply issue orders and expect them to be carried

Change processes doomed to failure	Successful change processes
• Change is driven by top management and is 'decreed from above'	• Change is a natural process that can be influenced by all employees
• The process is based on issuing orders and orders being obeyed	• Change process based on trust and cooperation
• Limited involvement of interested parties (works council, customers, partners, etc.)	• Intensive involvement of interested parties (works council, customers, partners, etc.)
• Limited awareness of the present situation	• Complete awareness of the present situation
• Focus on solving problems	• Focus on 'determining our own future'
• There is a vision, but it is not 'lived'	• Vision is understood and 'lived' by everyone
• Linear thinking	• System-oriented thinking
• One-way communication	• 360° communication
• Planning first, implementation second	• Simultaneous planning and implementation
• Mobilizing the top management	• Mobilizing all employees

Figure 8.3 Features of successful brand engagement initiatives
Source: Roland Berger Strategy Consultants

out. What this approach misses is the need for clear communication and education (so that staff know not only what the orders are generally, but how they relate specifically to their jobs), the development of the systems and processes that are necessary for staff to carry out these orders, and the motivation to do so. In fact, all three are related: positive involvement of those affected helps solve all three problems simultaneously.

When employees are involved in the process – with the ability to influence the outcome – not only are they likely to be much more motivated, they are also likely to input the practical know-how (and the work) needed to make day-to-day implementation possible.

Effective brand engagement depends on coordinated, disciplined activity on many fronts, simultaneously. These include:

◆ training and communication: making sure the right training and communications materials are produced, with the right message for each target audience (tone, style, level of detail and so on) at the right time via the right channel – so that every employee knows what he or she is expected to do, and why

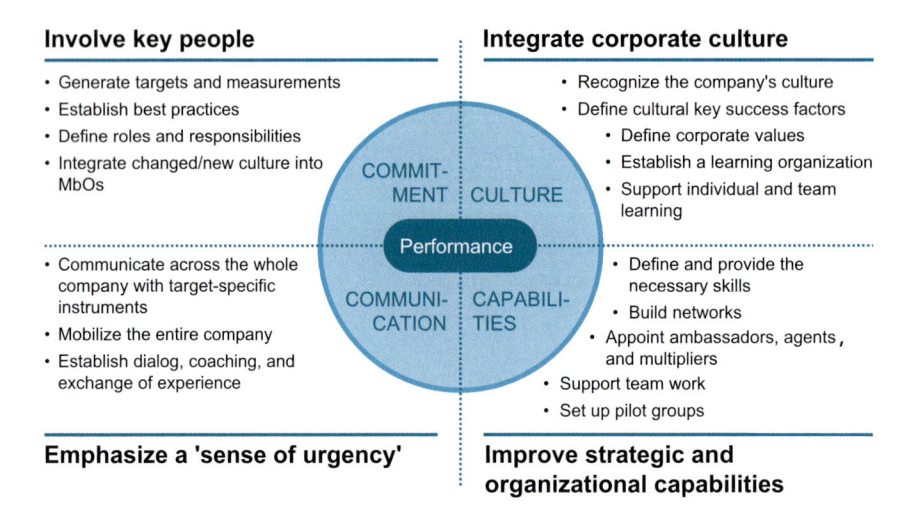

Involve key people

- Generate targets and measurements
- Establish best practices
- Define roles and responsibilities
- Integrate changed/new culture into MbOs

- Communicate across the whole company with target-specific instruments
- Mobilize the entire company
- Establish dialog, coaching, and exchange of experience

Emphasize a 'sense of urgency'

Integrate corporate culture

- Recognize the company's culture
- Define cultural key success factors
  - Define corporate values
  - Establish a learning organization
  - Support individual and team learning

  - Define and provide the necessary skills
  - Build networks
  - Appoint ambassadors, agents, and multipliers
  - Support team work
  - Set up pilot groups

Improve strategic and organizational capabilities

COMMIT-MENT · CULTURE

Performance

COMMUNI-CATION · CAPABILI-TIES

Figure 8.4 Effective change: a multi-layered, multi-faceted process
Source: Roland Berger Strategy Consultants

◆ rewards and incentives: aligning targets, measures, rewards, incentives, job descriptions, and promotions to encourage 'on-brand' behaviors while discouraging 'off-brand' behaviors

◆ operations and systems: making sure that staff have all the tools and supporting processes to do what they are supposed to do, efficiently and effectively

◆ culture and leadership: developing vision, commitment, and understanding so that employees not only know what they are supposed to be doing, they actually want to do it.

9 Tracking performance

Values-based brand management

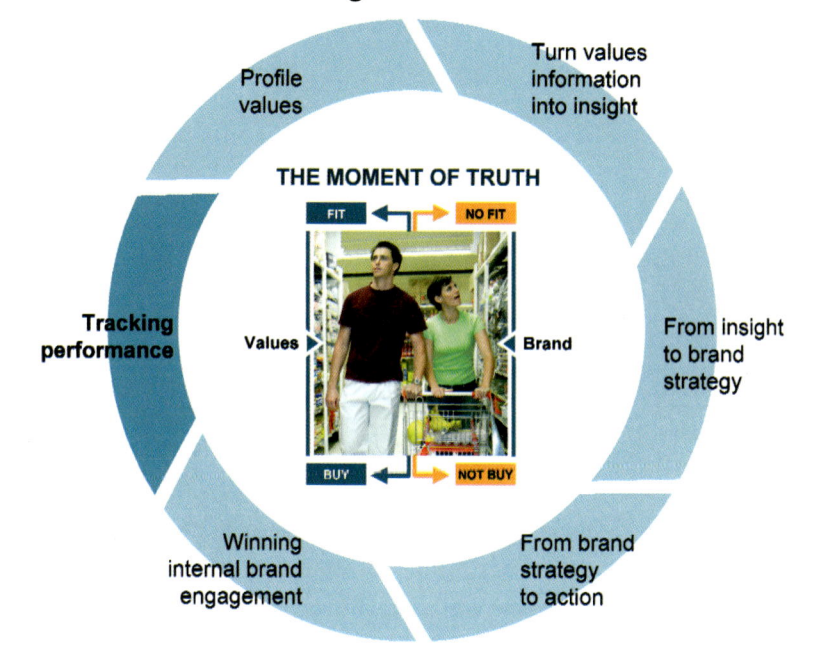

When we go to bed, overnight while we are sleeping, our car doesn't change very much. But the garden is alive with activity. Go on holiday for two weeks and when we come back the car is basically the same as when we left it. But the garden is overgrown.

The garden is organic. It keeps growing day and night. It is changing all the time. Markets are like gardens: organic, growing, and changing all the time. Good gardeners constantly tend their gardens.

Big changes are usually only needed as a result of neglect. If you overlook your garden for too long it gets so overgrown by weeds that you can't see the flowers. Precious plants die. Pests proliferate.

As in gardens, so with markets. Good marketers constantly tend their markets, forever on the look-out for significant change. If you ignore changes in your market, once-compelling offerings lose their luster, sales and margins suffer, and competitors crowd in. Insight, analysis, strategy formulation, disciplined execution – they are all wonderful things. But if they end up as just one-off projects, their real potential is still being squandered. Back in Chapter 7 we illustrated a good example of the importance of tracking. Yorn's core brand strategy was spot-on. But over time, day-to-day marketing initiatives failed to stay in line with this strategy. By tracking its performance the mistake could be identified and corrected before too much damage was done.

The secret of all successful businesses is momentum. And the secret of momentum, and of all successful marketing, is consistency – consistently aligning and realigning the brand to its market. That's why brand tracking is as crucial a part of the overall brand management as the original customer insight. Only by consistent brand tracking can we:

◆ ensure our marketing measures are moving in the right direction and achieving the desired results

◆ distinguish between very effective and less effective marketing activities

◆ identify shifts in the consumer base of the brand

◆ identify emerging opportunities and threats.

Things to look out for include:

◆ value/offer relative to the competition

◆ positioning relative to the competition

◆ changing priorities and preferences of core customers, not only in relation to the brand itself but in terms of shopping, media/communications, and so on

◆ checking who exactly is the competition

◆ changing technologies/cost structures.

Most successful brand managers already have sophisticated brand-tracking systems in place. What they do not have, however, is a mechanism for tracking the changing values of their customers: that is, whether the values of existing customers are actually changing, or whether the brand is attracting a different set of customers with a different values profile. Values research therefore needs to be incorporated, in a planned way, into the brand's ongoing research program – with at least an annual review to monitor changes. In addition, further detailed tracking work can be undertaken, via focus groups filtered into different archetypes, for example.

Good gardeners adjust their tracking and inspection processes to each element's natural rate of change. Half-hourly inspections of weed growth are a waste of time. But daily inspections may be necessary if a precious plant's new shoots are being attacked by slugs. Weekly may be all that's necessary to keep the weeds down or the lawn looking good. Yearly may be OK for the fence. Either way, values-monitoring systems need to be integrated into the organization's ongoing monitoring and tracking processes.

COCA-COLA CASE STUDY

In 2000, Coca-Cola's brand had lost much of its luster. An expert panel evaluated and established Coca-Cola's perceived value projection. Figure 9.1 shows only the values positively communicated by the Coca-Cola brand to the market – and they weren't much. There was some support for Passion. Thrill and fun and other hedonistic values hardly appeared at all, although the tendency towards Smart shopping suggested that Coke's ability to levy a price premium was in serious danger. The strongest value to appear – 24/7 pro-tech – was a value that Coca-Cola marketers had never intended to promote. As a consequence, Coca-Cola launched new marketing activities.

Eight months later, research conducted showed that the actual picture had not changed fundamentally, but it had begun to change (see Figure 9.2). The first thing to notice is that a contour had appeared around the values Passion, New and cool, and Customized, and there was no positive support for Smart shopping. Overall, the brand's profile still wasn't strong, but it was moving in the right direction.

Coca-Cola's projected value proposition, April 2000

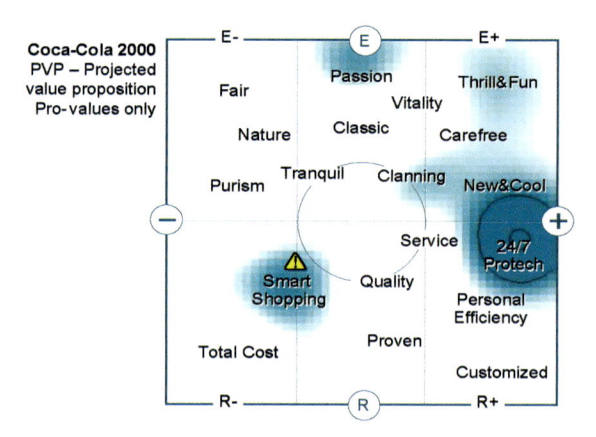

Figure 9.1 Coca-Cola's projected value proposition, Germany 2000
Source: Roland Berger Strategy Consultants, TNS Emnid data
(Germany, April 2000, n=1500, population 14–65 years, CATI)

Coca-Cola's actual value perception, January 2001

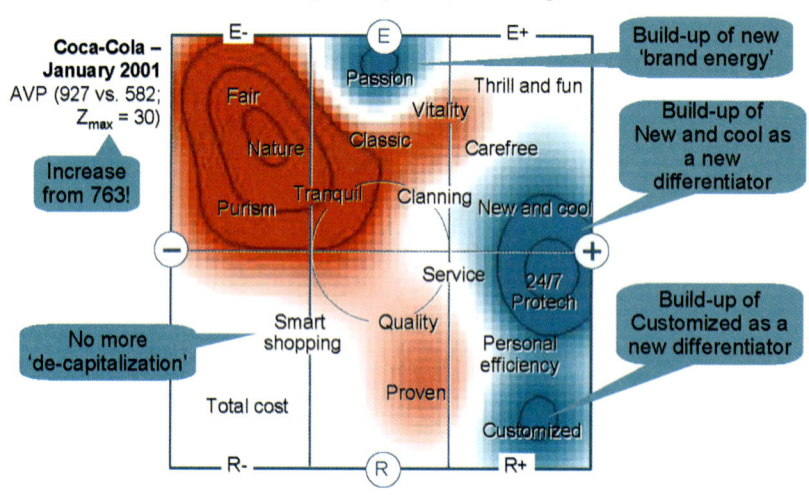

Figure 9.2 Tracking the effects of a Coca-Cola ad campaign
Source: Roland Berger Strategy Consultants, TNS Emnid data
(Germany, August 2001, n=1500, population 14–65 years, CATI)

SEVENONE CASE STUDY

SevenOne Media is the marketing and strategy center of the biggest commercial television family in Germany, the ProSiebenSat.1 Media AG, with four main channels. Sat1 is a mainstream channel with a widespread program schedule, competing head-to-head with the market leader RTL. ProSieben is a more up-market offering, providing first airings of major films and US blockbuster series such as *Friends* and *Desperate Housewives*. Kabel eins focuses more on classic movies and programs, while N24 is a 24-hour news channel.

The challenge facing SevenOne was how to use its portfolio of television stations to compete most effectively, especially against RTL. One channel alone would probably not be effective. But perhaps a combination of the different channels, each targeting a specific audience segment, might have a greater impact.

SevenOne decided to understand better and in a more systematic way the values of the users of its different channels – their actual value propositions.

Subsequent research (see Figure 9.3) showed that each station was good at attracting some archetypes and not so good at attracting others. For example, among ProSieben viewers, the archetypes Egotists and Maximalists were over-represented, while Altruists and Traditionalists were under-represented.

A previous analysis of the economic attractiveness of each archetype had identified the Egocentrists, Emotionalists, Maximalists, and Rationalists as the most attractive. The ProSieben station's performance among Egocentrics was excellent and it was good among Maximalists, though below par for the Emotionalists and Rationalists. It decided on a strategy that involved keeping the Egocentrics and improving its performance among the Maximalists and Rationalists. The Emotionalists were left to be one of the core archetypes of another family channel.

Using this methodology, SevenOne developed much more tightly focused TVPs for each of its main three channels (Sat1, ProSieben, and kabel eins). It then used these TVPs to fine-tune each channel's program schedule. Previously, executives working for Sat1 and ProSieben had often competed against each other for the same audiences and programs. Now they had a much clearer brief as to which programs fitted which channel's strategy.

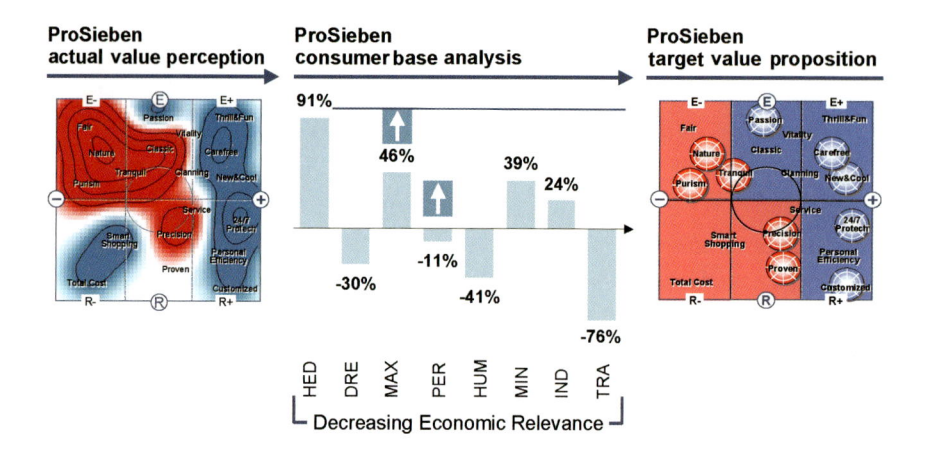

Figure 9.3 Identifying which archetypes for SevenOne to address via a new target value proposition
Source: Roland Berger Strategy Consultants

In this way, SevenOne was able to develop a 'pincer movement' on its arch-rival RTL.

But the initiative did not stop there. For SevenOne this is an on-going strategy that needs to be implemented afresh every day. So SevenOne has integrated the archetypes analysis and targeting into its ongoing research by fusing its data about its customer archetypes to the 'people meter' services offered by GfK Nürnberg, the research company serving the main television channels in Germany. This gives SevenOne information about how successfully each one of its programs is in attracting each archetype, every day (even second by second!). In this way, it can monitor how successful its targeting is, and identify the problem as soon as it starts straying off course.

Figure 9.5 shows a typical daily report which analyzes audience shares by age group, by program, and by archetype penetration. The color coding gives a quick 'at-a-glance' assessment of how well each program is performing. Overall, SevenOne's audiences are hugely over-represented among Egocentrists, Maximalists, and Minimalists, and under-represented among the other German archetypes. The color coding also quickly tells executive which particular programs are breaking out of this pattern.

152

	—Decreasing economic relevance for German consumer goods & services ⟶							
Archetype								
Name	Ego-centrics	Emo-tionalists	Maxi-malists	Ratio-nalists	Altru-ists	Mini-malists	Non-conformists	Tradi-tionalists
Size	5. 11%	1. 18%	4. 11%	3. 14%	2. 16%	6. 10%	8. 10%	7. 10%
Income	4.	8.	2.	1.	7.	6.	3.	5.
Affinity (MD) Private Television	1.	5.	3.	6.	7.	2.	4.	8.
Rating	1.	2.	3.	4.	5.	6.	7.	8.

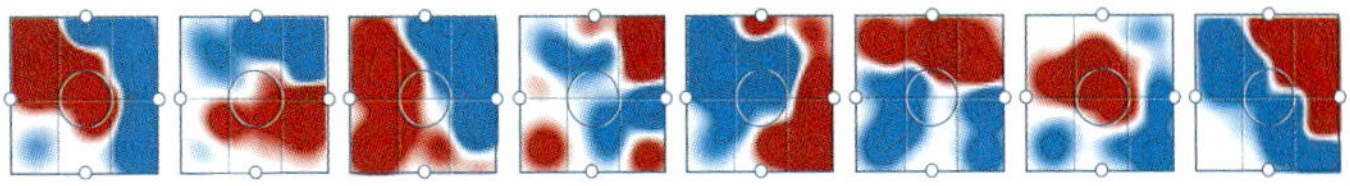

Base: Population 14+ years, Germany, n=1.508

Figure 9.4 Economic attractiveness of different archetypes to private television (Germany)
Source: Roland Berger Strategy Consultants, Forsa data, SevenOne Media, April 2004

This data gives executives a day-to-day feel for how well their strategy of attracting certain archetypes is panning out. Monthly and annual averages are reviewed and used for decision-making purposes.

Christian Schneiderbauer, Unit Director of Programme Research, is now working on the next iterations of this program. One key challenge, for example, is deciding which programs should run on which channels. Ideally each new program should fit each station's TVP, but how can this be assessed? One option is to employ panels of internal and external experts to analyze programs in much the same way that expert panels analyze the projected value propositions of television campaigns and other marketing materials (see Chapter 6). However, this is an expensive and time-consuming option, so Schneiderbauer is developing special focus groups to assess new programs. Some of these focus groups are being recruited by archetype – one focus group may be full of Maximalists, for example – while others are designed to reflect the population as a whole. In this way, Schneiderbauer hopes to predict the relative ability of different programs to attract different archetypes.

At the same time, SevenOne is seeking to match the actual value in order to deliver even more effective advertising to its advertisers.

Programs of previous day

Program	Time	shr% 14+	shr% 14-49	Ratio	Maxi.	Ego.	Altru.	Emot.	Non-Con.	Mini.	Tradit.
Will & Grace	13:13	6.7	11.1	45	170	184	60	66	88	167	39
Beverly Hills Beauties	13:41	7.2	11.9	71	154	193	75	68	89	132	31
Beastmaster	15:20	8.0	11.9	54	171	105	76	75	130	187	52
Relic Hunter	16:10	10.5	15.2	55	188	153	60	70	142	178	60
Die nervigsten Dinge der 90er	17:04	9.1	15.8	71	112	235	54	72	97	147	83
Terraluna	18:02	6.1	11.0	85	132	245	61	57	84	166	71
Welt der Wunder	19:02	5.7	10.1	94	133	159	70	62	92	232	37
ProSieben Nachrichten	20:00	4.6	8.3	131	129	160	76	59	80	194	31
Das fünfte Element	20:15	13.2	23.3	95	136	197	59	72	129	162	48
True Lies	22:52	14.0	20.4	75	129	163	66	74	98	166	40

▨ >121   ☐ 80–120   ■ 0–79

Index: Market Share (shr) adults 14+ = 100   Base: All TV-households Germany (D+EU)

Figure 9.5 ProSieben's daily tracking of audience shares, by archetype
Source: Roland Berger Strategy Consultants/AGF/GfK Fernsehforschung/SevenOne
Media

Using its understanding of audience values, SevenOne Media has managed to create much stronger internal cohesion and sense of direction, while developing a strategy whose implementation it can monitor and adjust day to day, thanks to its ongoing audience monitoring. Market shares and advertising revenues are rising and executives are confident that better targeting is part of the explanation for these rising trends.

SUMMARY

Research, analysis, insight, strategy development, implementation – it's all hard work and it can be expensive. It's tempting to leave brand tracking as an afterthought as 'an additional expense we would rather do without.' Gardeners are often tempted not to tend their gardens, too. That's when things get out of control. Without monitoring and review, mistakes will not be noticed, opportunities not identified, and ultimately learning will not take place. But that is what effective brand management is all about: continuous learning about markets and customers. Consistent, disciplined brand tracking is an essential part of the overall brand management process.

10   Issues and questions

Over the last chapters we have made many claims for a values-based approach to brand management. Does that mean it's a panacea? Of course not. Every methodology has its limits and pitfalls.

To work properly, for example, a values-based approach usually requires fresh research. To make sure our Ariadne-thread doesn't break half-way through the process, we need to conduct new research connecting customers' values to their demographics, purchasing preferences, behaviors, and so on. This is an upfront cost which many companies would prefer not to pay. While it is possible to 'reverse engineer' existing data onto new values research, the results will never be as rich or accurate as research specifically designed for this purpose. Taking a strategic approach does have budgetary implications.

The values approach is also statistical. It does not identify the values of every customer, only statistically representative samples. It is not therefore designed to streamline or enrich 'one-to-one' marketing programs such as customer relationship management. Of course, it is theoretically possible to append individual values data to each customer's transaction and behavioral histories (assuming customers are prepared to complete the research), but it is not clear that the benefits would outweigh the costs.

There are also some areas where a values-based approach seems less applicable – or at least, works in less obvious ways.

'DEMOCRATIC' BRANDS

At first sight, some brands appear to contradict the evidence in this book. We call them 'democratic brands.'

Democratic brands have such high market penetrations that any analysis of their user base – of the category or the brand – tends to mirror that of the population as a whole. Values profiles, remember, measure the difference between the user base and the population. In this case there is very little difference, so the values profile gives us very little new information. No values stand out as brand differentiators. Figure 10.1 shows an example from the German banking market. There are no statistically significant contour lines: the values of bank users are basically the same as those of the population generally.

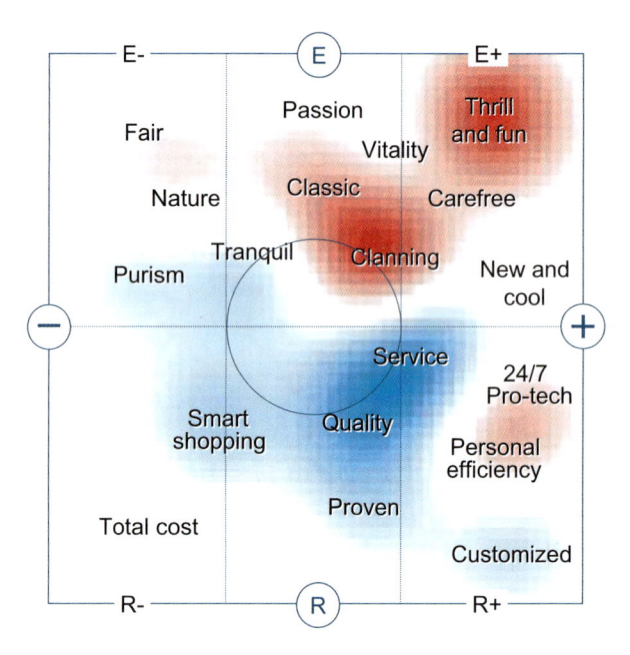

Figure 10.1 Values profile of bank users in Germany
Source: Roland Berger Strategy Consultants, Roland Berger Market Research data (Germany, March 2005, n=2004, population 16–69 years, CATI)

Many big brands operating in utility-style categories follow this pattern, including banking, grocery retailing, fixed-line telephony, and petrol retailing. They sell necessities that everyone has to buy, so their values profiles are similar to those of the population as a whole. And because people treat them as necessities – 'things I have to get out of the way so that I can get on with my life' – they are rarely seen as instruments of personal expression. You may seek to express your values via the car you drive, but you are less likely to do so through the petrol you put in it. Does this mean values-based analysis is irrelevant for these brands?

In one sense, democratic brands are wrestling with a problem most brand managers would love to have. Because they are purchased by so many people, their customer bases tend to be bigger than any single values group or archetype. As Table 10.1 shows, even the biggest archetype (in this case, in Germany) accounts for less than 20 percent of the population: most brands would be very happy with a 20 percent share. But there are some brands with much higher shares, and this raises a dilemma for them: where is future growth going to come from?

One option is to grow by expanding market share within the brand's existing territory. Another option is to grow by addressing the same values groups across many different territories. Nike is an example of this second approach. As we showed back in Chapter 5 (page

Table 10.1 German archetypes as percentages of the population

Archetype	% of total population
Performer	18.6
Humanists	16.5
Maximalists	13.9
Dreamers	12.5
Hedonists	9.3
Minimalists	8.8
Traditionalists	8.4
Individualists	7.9

Note: 4.2 percent cannot be classified because of value discrepancies.

79), it has expanded globally, appealing to the same values groups in each new territory. Knowingly or otherwise, it has adopted a values-based growth strategy.

Big brands seeking to expand their presence within the same territorial population have a bigger challenge, as illustrated by Figure 10.2. In Chapter 4 we also discussed the trade-offs that brands are forced to make as they grow: between higher market penetration and increased differentiation. Generally speaking, it is very difficult to build high levels of brand mass without losing the distinctiveness that gives the brand energy. The perfect best-of-both-worlds tiger very rarely happens in practice. An invisible barrier – the trade-offs represented by the diagonal line – stops most brands reaching it.

Democratic brands lie at the extreme right hand of this trade-off line. For them, any attempt to become more distinctive is likely to put off some customers and actually lead to a fall in sales and market share. The brand appears trapped in a lowest common denominator commodity mindset and market. Indeed, seeking to build greater brand energy might seem counter-productive. The very scale delivered by the democratized brand – the high volumes, low unit costs, huge

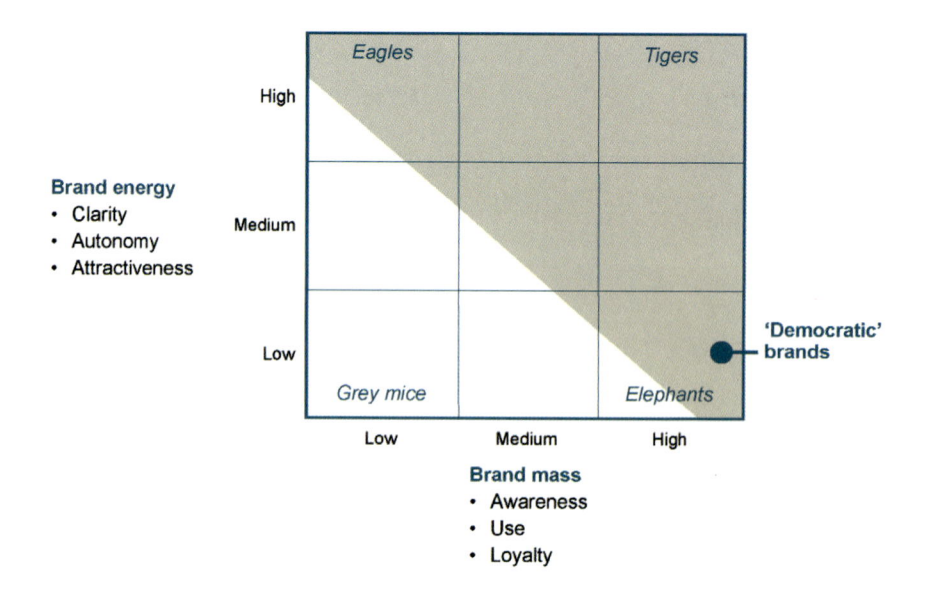

Figure 10.2 The challenge for 'democratic' brands
Source: Roland Berger Strategy Consultants

installed base – may give it significant competitive advantage in the form of market muscle which acts as an important barrier to entry. In petrol retailing for example, where most buyers simply buy on the basis of which petrol station is the closest, the key to market share lies in having as many retail outlets as possible in the best locations. In these cases, then, 'targeting everyone' – opting not to target specific values groups or archetypes – may seem to be the best way forward: 'the blander the better.'

But is this really a valid conclusion? In some rare situations it may be: former public sector monopolies spring to mind.

But in most cases the influence of values does show through. Figure 10.3 shows a joint space analysis of the German retail banking market, for example. Most bank brands are clustered in the middle: their values profile is very similar to the average of the population as a

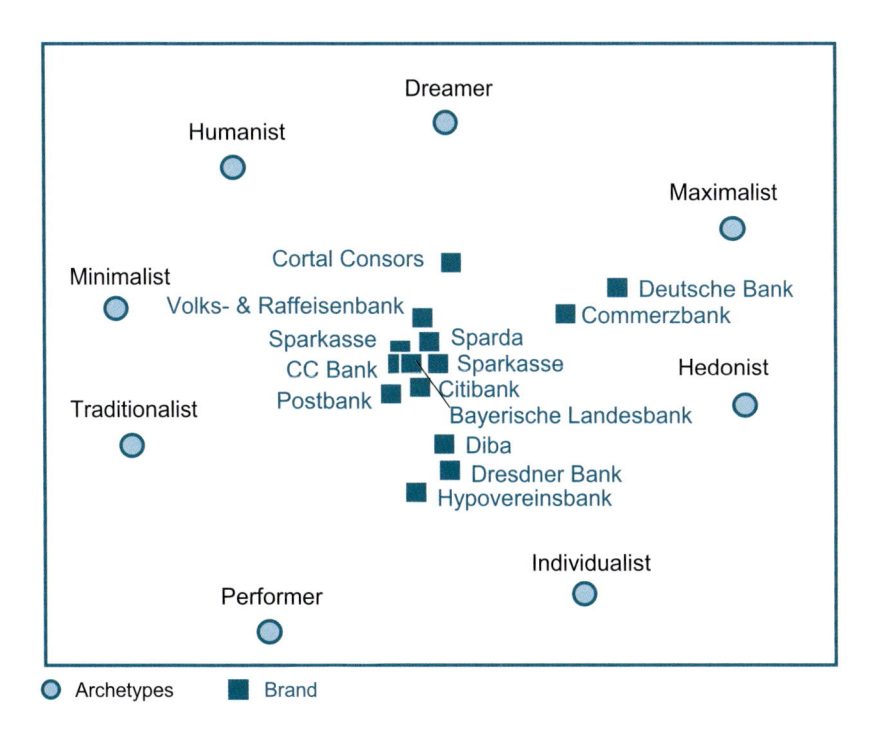

Figure 10.3 Mapping bank brands against value archetypes
Source: Roland Berger Strategy Consultants, Roland Berger Market Research data (Germany, March 2005, n=2004, population 16–69 years, CATI)

whole. But some brands do appeal to some archetypes more than others. Deutsche Bank and Commerzbank are much closer to Maximalists, for example; Dresdner Bank and Hypovereinsbank are closer to Individualists and Performers; while Cortal Consors is closer to Dreamers, with a more emotional focus.

The box gives a reminder of some of the attributes of these archetypes. Translated into different types and styles of banking service, these archetypes clearly have important implications. The opportunity for greater differentiation is clearly there. If a number of more differentiated brands did emerge in this market, they could expose the lowest common denominator nature of most democratized brands. More highly differentiated brands could target and 'siphon off' specific values groups. Attacked from many sides, the democratic brand has only one way to go in terms of market share: down.

Archetypes: a reminder

Maximalists tend to be relatively affluent, seeing premium brands as an important mechanism of self-expression. They are prepared to invest a great deal in their way of living – and reject any form of renunciation or asceticism. **Individualists** tend to focus on pragmatic and functional aspects of products rather than on brands. They are more interested in machines and theories than in other people – they are always eager to use the newest technologies. **Dreamers** reject performance orientations, including innovative technologies. They are not very disciplined and do not focus on efficiency or quality. They simply want to enjoy life and not bother too much about the future.

How can democratic brands respond to this challenge? One possibility is to analyze and target customers in a more finely tuned way, by focusing on heavy versus light users, for example, or different usage profiles. For example, most people drink at least a little Coca-Cola, so the values profile of Coke's user base is pretty 'white.' However, the values profile of its younger, heavy users may be much more distinctive: defining the parameters of research, and being open-minded and curious about the data, are crucial.

Likewise in petrol retailing, an analysis of the values of specific user groups such as taxi drivers and commercial salespeople might reflect strong profiles worth targeting with specific offerings. Similarly, different types of user might display different values. What about net borrowers versus net savers in banking, for example? Digging deeper in this way may reveal opportunities for specific marketing initiatives – perhaps even sub-brands – aimed at different segments. In the United Kingdom, for instance, the market-leading grocery retailer Tesco prides itself on being a democratic brand that appeals to the 'average' UK consumer. At the same time, however, it has a wide range of segmented offerings, all hanging under the umbrella brand Tesco, including a 'Finest' range for gourmet shoppers, a 'Value' range for the price conscious, healthy eating ranges, and so on.

INNOVATION

Technically speaking, it is impossible to conduct values-based research on brand new products or services. Analyzing market drivers means understanding the values of the people who are active in that market, which is not possible if it is a brand new market. Does that mean values-based analysis has little to offer when it comes to innovation?

The first thing to note is that values-based analysis is not the only methodology to struggle with novelty. Market research generally is notoriously bad at divining which new products or services will succeed or fail in the future. Indeed, marketing folklore is full of stories of market researchers' failures to anticipate consumers' responses to innovations and inventions. If Sony had listened to its researchers, it would have never launched the Sony Walkman. Not a single mobile phone operator predicted the runaway success of text messaging.

Nevertheless values-based analysis can aid innovation in two ways. First, when bringing a new product or service to market, it can help identify which target audiences are most likely to be attracted to the new offering, and how to communicate its benefits. It's no great surprise for example that mobile phones are used most by people attracted strongly to the values 24/7 pro-tech and Personal efficiency. An organic food range is much more likely to appeal to Humanists and

Dreamers, who are big on values like Fair and Nature. Given our understanding of the shopping and media consumption habits of these different values groups, values analysis can help fine-tune the positioning of new products and new brands – message content – while also influencing the details of message delivery: how, when, and where (see Chapter 6).

The second way values-based analysis can help is by identifying market gaps to spur future innovation. Figure 10.4 shows a joint space analysis from a project in Portugal where three major brands were battling it out for market share. Remember, joint space analysis places different values archetypes on a map depending on how close, or distant, they are from each other. Archetypes with values that are sharply opposed are placed at opposite ends of the map; archetypes that are similar nestle more closely together. In this case, Minimalists

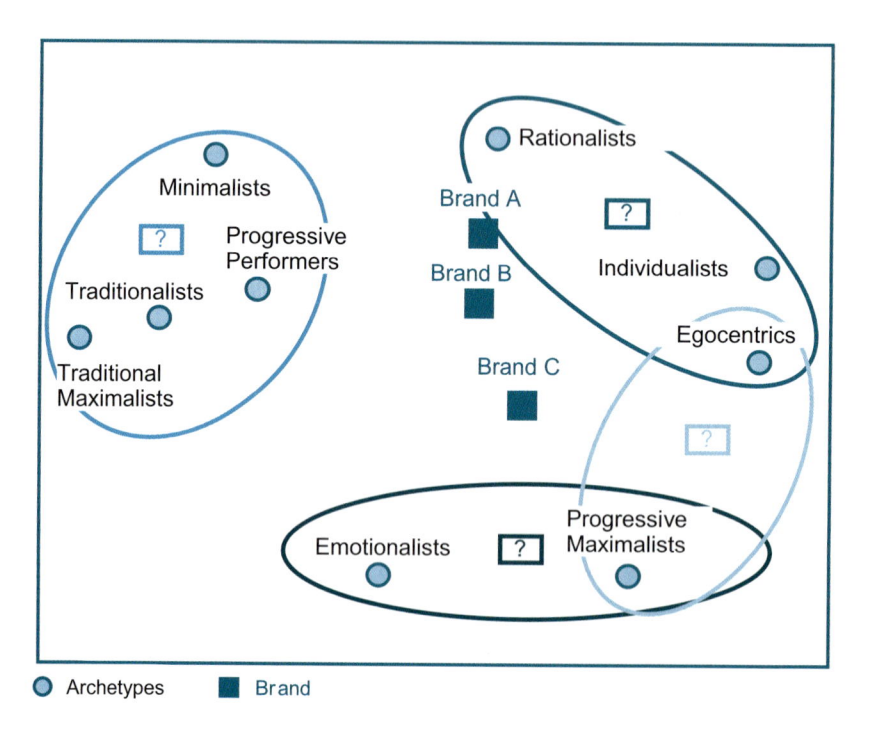

Figure 10.4 How joint space analysis reveals market gaps
Source: Roland Berger Strategy Consultants, Metris data (Portugal, June 2004, n=2650, population 12–65 years, CATI)

are quite similar to Progressive performers but very different from Progressive maximalists. (The Portuguese consumer archetypes are shown in Figure 3.11, page 57.)

In this particular market, the three main brands all cluster relatively closely: in the middle. There are some differences. Brand A is clearly attracting more Rationalists than Brand C, which is much closer to Egocentrics and Progressive maximalists. But as the question marks show, in theory at least, there are many other possible positionings that could create much more highly differentiated brands.

Arguably, for example, a new brand or offering entering the map at the top left-hand corner could make four archetypes all its own (Minimalists, Progressive performers, Traditionalists, and Traditional maximalists). The common feature of all these archetypes is that they major on values like Fair, Nature, Quality, and Proven, while actively rejecting values such as Thrill and fun and New and cool.

Down at the bottom right-hand corner, another brand/offering could attract two very different archetypes (Progressive maximalists and Emotionalists). They major on values such as Passion, Vitality, and Thrill and fun. Meanwhile a brand or product addressing the Rationalists, Individualists, and Egocentrics could major on values such as 24/7 pro-tech and Personal efficiency. When we map how close existing brands are to the key archetypes or values groups, potential gaps in the market are made clear for all to see. Marketers could 'work backwards' from the market gaps to dream up completely new propositions covering both product and service attributes and communication platforms.

Please note, such gap analysis is just the first step of any successful innovation strategy. Gap analysis simply pinpoints a possibility that requires further analysis. There may be good reasons why no brand is targeting these archetypes. They may not be economically attractive. We saw an example of this back in Chapter 6, where Accor decided to focus on only four of eight German archetypes, because four of them were infrequent, low spenders.

If the identified archetypes do prove to be economically attractive, however, the joint space analysis can speed us along the process of identifying what sort of product, services, and appeals we need to develop. This doesn't avoid the risk of innovation. But it does provide a strategic filter and a powerful direction-setting mechanism.

BUILDING GLOBAL BRANDS

Another key challenge for many brand owners is the development of international or global brands. The problems here have been well aired. Even if the product is the same the world over (it may not be), customers differ, and historical brand positionings differ too. One man's meat is often another man's poison, so a brand positioning that works well in one region might not work well at all in another. The attempt to appeal to everyone everywhere can lead to lowest-common-denominator solutions: global blands rather than global brands.

Or else, the attempt to 'think global, act local' means that costs, confusion, and complexity multiply as marketers in different localities develop different brand positionings for different markets. When Adidas studied its product profile across Europe, for example, it discovered that just 3 percent of its portfolio was common to all European markets. Staying outstandingly relevant to local markets while building a common, global platform is often like trying to square a circle.

Can a values-based approach help address these dilemmas? The tentative answer is Yes.

The first thing values-based analysis can do is help to identify when a 'global' or a 'local' positioning is most relevant. If the values of the local sets of users in territory A and territory B are very different, then the chances of building a global brand on the same communications platform are slim. Values analysis can therefore help identify when a global brand strategy is a viable option and when it is not.

It can also help implementation. The extra ingredient added by values analysis is a by-product of its methodology: every profile is *relative*. There is no such thing as an absolute profile in values analysis. Every profile depicts the differences in values between a sub-set of a population and the population as a whole. A value only shows up as red or blue if the sample concerned is more attracted to, or repelled by, that particular value *than the specific population it is being measured against*. If you change either the sub-set or the population you get a different profile. It's one thing to compare Audi users against the population 'all car users,' for example. It's another thing to compare the same Audi users against 'all new car users,' or 'all *luxury* car users.'

Let's say, for example, that the population as a whole in Japan scores '2' on the value New and cool, and a specific segment scores

'3.' In this case, the value New and cool will appear blue on a values profile of the segment, because it is more attracted to New and cool than its reference group. Now let's say that the population as a whole in Korea scores '5' on New and cool. This means that the population as a whole is much 'Newer and cooler' than the Japanese population, including the New and cool Japanese segment. However, there might be a specific segment of the Korean population that scores '6' on New and cool. This segment is Newer and cooler than the average, so its profile also appears blue because it scores higher than the average. Should this happen, the values profiles of the two segments in Korea and Japan would come out exactly the same. Both blue; both Newer and cooler than their peers in their local markets – *even though their absolute degrees of Newness and coolness differ.*

Fascinatingly, this is exactly what happens with many global brands. The evidence so far suggests that global brands are often best built by stressing the *relative* differences between local target groups and their local populations – and repeating this relative difference across the globe – rather than by creating an absolute, single uniform 'global' brand execution which is presented exactly the same way in every territory.

When Roche Diagnostics analyzed its users across a whole series of territories from the United States to Japan, for example, it discovered that in absolute terms, the values of these users were different. However, a closer inspection also revealed that in each country, compared with their local populations, users of the Roche brand were more inclined to values such as Quality and Proven than the average. Even though customer values differed across different territories, the customers differed from their local populations in similar ways. It was this that gave Roche the confidence to develop cobas® as a global rather than regional or national brand: it had a springboard for a Quality, Proven positioning in every market it operated in.

In another case, a global cosmetics company presented its brand in two territories in exactly the same way. In one territory it was extremely successful, but in the other territory its market share declined inexorably. Values analysis showed why. Consumer values in the two markets were very different. Target users in one territory were far more attracted to values such as Passion, Vitality, and Thrill and fun than they were in the other. Marketing campaigns that seemed passionate, vital, and thrilling to one audience seemed dull and bland to the other audience. Having recognized this, the company was able to tweak its communications accordingly. The brand's core, global positioning remained absolutely intact. But now marketers knew they needed to express this core positioning differently in order to fit conditions in each local market. After they did so, the market share decline reversed.

Key learnings

- ◆ 'Democratic' brands with large numbers of users reflecting the values of the population as a whole need to dig deeper into their customer bases to identify the brand's driving values.

- ◆ Joint space mapping can help direct innovation by highlighting values segments that are currently under-served within the marketplace.

- ◆ Values analysis helps to identify the similarities and differences between brand users across nations and regions. Often, even where the absolute differences are significant, the relative differences are small. This provides a good foundation for the development of a global brand.

SUMMARY

A values-based approach to brand management requires upfront investment. It also needs to be applied creatively to situations such as 'democratic' brands whose user bases reflect the population as a whole and when introducing new products and services. Application of the methodology to global brands has been tested, but is nevertheless in its infancy – though there is evidence that the approach has rich potential.

But we still have a lot to learn. Nowhere is this more so than in the challenge closest to home – the internal one of creating an organization with the culture, structures, and processes to make brand management a truly strategic task. We discuss this in our concluding chapter.

11 The CEO's moment of truth

Top-line growth, higher margins, greater competitive advantage: better brand management is not a complete answer to any one of these ever-present challenges, but it is part of the answer to all of them.

Strategic brand management helps set the direction for the entire organization, orienting it positively towards markets and customers while also facilitating disciplined, effective execution. But the challenge of better brand management goes deep. Most brand management today is not strategic. Instead it's plagued by common misunderstandings about how brands work and where superior margins come from. Phoney opposites continue to divert practitioners. Is marketing and branding a creative or analytic process? Is it just external gloss or a strategic input? Is it about appealing to people's emotions or delivering hard, tangible product and cost benefits?

In addition, too many brand programs get lost in the market maze discussed in Chapter 1 and brands are managed in a fragmented way. Issues of value alignment – which revolve around product and service attributes, pricing, operations, and R&D – are handled by different people, using different processes and different metrics from those dealing with external communications aspects. The net result is major disconnects between 'strategy' and 'tactics,' between operations and communications, between marketers and their corporate peers: poor coordination and poor execution lead to poor performance.

But this is not the fault of the marketing department. It represents a strategic, organizational, and structural failure.

In this book we have outlined a different approach to brand management, an approach which overcomes or avoids many of these problems, which are by-products of marketing's 'product push' history. The alternative approach requires that we enter the marketing maze from a different starting point: starting not with the product and its attributes, or even customers and their specific functional 'needs,' but with the *person* and his or her *values*. Everything else follows from this different point of departure (see Figure 11.1).

Only if we have understood people's values can we then understand how these values are made manifest in their product, service, and communication preferences, and the emotions which color their judgments.

The value Smart shopping is not just about 'rational' price competition, for example. It is also about the emotions of being smart: not having the wool pulled over your eyes; the thrill of the bargain hunt. If we understand the values of Dr Karl Bergmann and Jan, then we can divine what products and services they will want, what emotions they will bring to these products and services, and what communications they will respond to (see Figure 11.2). The

Figure 11.1 Strategic brand management starts from a different place
Source: Roland Berger Strategy Consultants

Figure 11.2 Values provide a holistic understanding of customer preferences
Source: Roland Berger Strategy Consultants

values-based approach to brand management therefore provides us with the insight that creates a seamless connection between the emotional and the rational, the product attribute and the communication. It helps create the moment of truth that leads to purchase.

But values-based analysis does more than deliver us the insights that help build great brands. Because it is based on hard, robust data that connects each individual's values data to his or her demographic details, product usage, shopping habits, media consumption habits, and so on, it also assists implementation down to the finest details of, say, media buying. The *same* analysis generates insights *and* helps implement them. This makes marketing *both* more efficient and more effective.

In addition, because different values groups are attracted to different brands (as we've seen) it also helps address more complex 'meta-problems' of brand portfolio and architecture. Thus it creates a powerful link between strategy and tactics.

It also works internally as well as externally. It turns hard data into easy-to-understand visuals that help create a common language for all those involved. It helps employees and business partners understand what they are trying to do, and why.

This general approach is applicable to *both* consumer and B2B markets. Different businesses have different values that shape their decisions, and effective marketing understands and addresses these values. A B2B company that values Precision and Excellence, for example, tends to behave very differently from one that values Innovation or Solidity. A business that values Total ownership cost is different from one that values Purchase price. It is as important to understand these values in business relationships as it is to understand them in consumer relationships (as we saw in the case of the commodity chemicals producer).

A values-based approach to brand management also helps set strategic direction and encourage focused innovation. It's an occupational disease for producers to get fixated with their products' attributes. Once upon a time Sony's Walkman was new and cool. Then MP3 players became new and cool. The underlying value New and cool didn't change, but how it was made manifest and addressed did. Companies that focus on product attributes while losing sight of the values they express forever risk being left behind by the markets they serve. Only by continually 'jumping' between the two levels – underlying values and specific manifestations – can we keep aligned to our markets to keep on delivering moments of truth, one moment after another.

THE CEO AGENDA

But none of this can happen if brand management is left to an isolated marketing department. The Ariadne-thread we've talked about in this book has to work its way through many different departments and specialisms, to unite and align them all. The approach to brand management we have talked about – a strategic approach – is a major cross-functional challenge embracing:

♦ Setting the organization's direction: which markets and which customers are we going to address and how?

♦ Operations: delivering the right products and services for the identified target markets at the right price.

♦ R&D and innovation: continually realigning value propositions to best address targeted values.

◆ Channel strategy: making these value propositions available via the customer's preferred channels.

◆ Human resources: training and motivating staff so that they deliver the right brand experience, consistently, at every touch point.

◆ Communications strategy: making sure the right messages get through to the right people, via the channels and media they prefer, at the lowest possible cost.

Making strategic brand management happen therefore is the CEO's moment of truth: confronting the organizational, structural, and cultural implications.

Organizations that are organized around products tend to lose sight of their customers. Banks, for example, are traditionally organized around product silos, with one division delivering current accounts, another delivering loans or savings, and yet another offering credit cards. Marketers working within each division naturally focus on 'the market' for each of their products, each one of them seeking to identify, target, and reach good prospects.

Even if the same individual buys all four products he or she remains invisible because the data is held in product silos which don't 'talk' to each other. Likewise, a consumer products company like Procter & Gamble is organized around many different product-based divisions: hair care, skin care, baby care, fabric care, surface cleaning (floors, dishes, and so on), dental care, and so on. Once again, the same individual may buy many of these products, but this information may not be visible to marketers working in each separate division.

Companies that organize themselves around product silos in this way forever risk becoming so product-focused that they end up not being customer-focused. That is why overcoming these divisions has become such an important agenda over the last few years. Banks have invested immense effort in trying to get different product-oriented databases to 'talk' to each other to create a single customer view. Procter & Gamble's 'golden household' project sought to identify those households that buy not just one P&G brand but many P&G brands. In each case, marketers hope that focusing better on the customer rather than the product will lead to more efficient, effective marketing.

The implications of this book take us one step further down this road. In the old days, the product defined the brand, and the brand then presented the product's attributes to the customer. The approach we have described here turns this process on its head. Branding starts with the person, not the product. The consumer's values define the brand, and the brand then presents these values to the company, requiring the company to construct a particular mix of product, service, distribution, and communication attributes to fit the demands of the brand. In this way the brand works its way 'inside' the organization – ultimately to change the way it works and organizes itself.

It's a well-known insight that structure should follow strategy. Values-based brand management takes this one step further: structure follows brand, brand follows strategy. Once it has been defined which values it is going to appeal to, everything about the organization – its structures, priorities, technical skills, operational requirements, even culture – needs to be aligned to this core purpose.

What is needed is a 'chief brand officer' role – an authoritative, senior position capable of bringing together all the necessary specialisms and functions to deliver the brand's requirements. In some cases, the CEO might take on this role. In other cases, a separate role might be needed. Either way, the central strategic importance needs to be recognized in organizational structures and reporting lines. Brand management needs to become a strategic process.

Technical appendix

The strategic brand management approach described in this book is based on a rigorous quantitative methodology, the individual components of which are summarized below.

VALUES

The values analyzed are taken to be latent variables. That is, individuals are never directly asked to judge the importance of a specific value. Rather, attitudinal statements relating to these values are taken as surrogate measurements. The importance of a value for an individual or a company is then obtained as a weighted sum of three to six statements relating to this value.

GEOGRAPHY

The arrangement of the values on the two-dimensional plane is obtained by performing a multi-dimensional scaling analysis of the values measured. The result is a rotationally invariant solution which places values with positive correlation in proximity to each other while leaving negatively correlated values at a greater distance. The overall solution is optimal in a mathematical sense: that all pairwise differences come closest to mirroring the true correlation relationships of all values involved.

PROFILES

Profiles of individuals, or of groups of individuals or companies, are computed based on point-wise t-tests for differences in means for the values analyzed. The results of these point-wise test statistics are then smoothed spatially to account for the importance of geographic proximity.

Areas shaded in blue indicate those values on which the individual or group places higher importance than the reference group (most often the population average). Conversely, areas shaded in red indicate values on which the individual or group places less importance than the reference group.

Differences significant at a significance level of 95 percent are bounded by the outermost contour line. Statistically speaking this means that the likelihood of observing purely by chance a difference within at least the first contour line is smaller than 5 percent. Multiple layers of contour lines indicate increasing significance levels, and thus even smaller probabilities of chance observance. Shaded areas outside the contour lines indicate differences not significant at the 95 percent level. For these differences, the probability of observing them purely by chance is larger than 5 percent.

ARCHETYPES

Archetypes are obtained by hierarchical (agglomerative) clustering of all individuals in the reference population. All values but no other dimensions are used for clustering. The preferred number of clusters is chosen primarily by an elbow criterion, judging loss of resolution when moving to fewer clusters.

JOINT SPACE MAPPING

Joint space mapping plots archetypes (segments of the population) and user groups (brands) on a two-dimensional plane, where the axes become essentially irrelevant. Using a Euclidean distance model and multi-dimensional scaling, archetypes of similar value structures will appear close together; opposing archetypes will be far apart. Brands or other user groups are then simply plotted onto this plane by using an orthogonal projection based on the archetype proportions in the specific user group. This means that if a specific group were to consist solely of one archetype, this group would be plotted directly on top of this archetype. A group consisting more or less evenly of each archetype will appear roughly in the center of the graph at more or less equal distance to all archetypes.